RIGHT
WHERE YOU ARE
SITTING NOW

The nature of things is in the habit
of concealing itself.

Heraclitus (Fragment 123)

RIGHT
WHERE YOU ARE
SITTING NOW

Further Tales of the Illuminati

Robert Anton Wilson

RONIN
www.roninpub.com

Right Where You Are Sitting Now
ISBN: 978-0-914171-45-4
Copyright © 1982, 1992 by Robert Anton Wilson
Second Edition 1992

Published by
RONIN Publishing, Inc.
PO BOX 22900
OAKLAND CA 94609
www.roninpub.com

Project Editors: Sebastian Orfali, Carlene Schnabel
Manuscript Editors: Peter Beren, Jim Schreiber, Dzintar Dravneiks
Cover: Matthew Gouig, Sebastian Orfali, Eugene Mosier
Illustrations: Matthew Gouig
Design and Pasteup: Sueellen Ehnebuske, Elizabeth Hillegass
Typesetting: Richard Ellington

U.S. Library of Congress Cataloging in Publication Data
Wilson, Robert Anton, 1932-
      Right where you are sitting now
        1. Occult Sciences, I. Title

PERMISSIONS
p. 13, "Deadly Nightshade" first appeared in *Gallery* (1971)
p. 67, "The Persecution and Assassination of the Parapsychologists as Performed by the Inmates of the American Association for the Advancement of Science under the Direction of The Amazing Randi" first appeared in *High Times* (August, 1980).
p. 105, "Bucky Fuller Synergistic Savior" first appeared in *Science Digest* (November, 1981). Copyright 1981 by the Hearst Corporation.
p. 127, "The Semantics of 'God'" first appeared in *The Realist* (May, 1959)
p. 135, "Ecology and Conspiracy" first appeared in *Critique: A Quarterly Journal Exploring Conspiracy Theories, Metaphysics, and the 'American Culture'* (Spring, 1981)
p. 169, "Hedonic Engineering and the Future of Sex" first appeared in *Oui* (1976).

Printed in the United States of America
Distributed by Publishers Group West

To
William S. Burroughs
and
Philip K. Dick
Pioneers

EMPEROR

LIVE LIKE HIM

Endorsed by the Illuminati

NORTON

Joshua Norton, or as he preferred to be called, Norton I, proclaimed himself Emperor of the United States and Protector of Mexico in 1859.

Although a pauper, he was fed free in San Francisco's best restaurants.

Although a madman, he had all his state proclamations published in San Francisco's newspapers.

While rational reformers elsewhere failed to crack the national bank monopoly with alternate currency plans, Norton I had his own private currency accepted throughout San Francisco.

When the Vigilantes decided to have a pogrom against the Chinese, and sane men would have tried to stop them, Norton I did nothing but stand in the street, head bowed, praying. The Vigilantes dispersed.

"When the proper man does nothing (wu-wei), his thought is felt ten thousand miles." —Lao Tse

Although a fool, Norton I wrote letters which were seriously considered by Abraham Lincoln and Queen Victoria.

"You must take the bull by the tail and look the facts in the face."
—W.C. Fields

Although a charlatan, Norton I was so beloved that 30,000 people turned out for his funeral in 1880.

"Everybody understands Mickey Mouse. Few understand Hermann Hesse. Hardly anybody understands Einstein. And nobody understands Emperor Norton."
—Malaclypse the Younger, K.S.C.

Discordian Society

A Bridge between Pisces and Aquarius

Text by Robert Anton Wilson
Sacred Chao symbol originated by Gregory Hill

TABLE OF CONTENTS

CONTACT
HAS BEEN
MADE

DEADLY NIGHTSHADE

Sure I'll make a statement but you'll have a lot of trouble understanding it. Maybe I was born to be hanged, but then again maybe not. You might say that things just piled up on me. The Zionist Proctoscopes and the flying saucer and all those sensuous people with their vibrators. Okay, I'll try to keep it orderly. My name is James Tyrone Carpenter, but you can call me Jim; everybody does. I been sheriff here in Mad Dog and Mad Dog County, in the great state of Texas, for nineteen years. My poor wife was named Suzie Belle. No kids—but the doc says she's the one who can't. We're what folks here call Yeller Dog Democrats; that is, we vote the straight party ticket even if there's a old yeller hound dog on it. Yes, and even if the Republicans were running Jesus Christ that year. Daddy was a dirt farmer and so was his daddy before him. Folks trust me. No, don't hurry me. I am getting to the point, in my own way. I saw the flying saucer fifteen years ago . . . Damn it, the flying saucer is connected. If you don't want to let me tell my own story in my own words— Well, okay, I decided to kill Suzie Belle about a month ago. Because of the sensuous people. What? That's what I been trying to tell you. If you let me tell it in my own way, it would all make sense like the multiplication table. The flying saucer—

They don't teach you much manners in that highfalutin college, do they? Won't let a body talk at all. Okay, then. It really all started with the Proctoscopes of the Elderly Zionists. My daddy read about them in a fine patriotic magazine put out by Reverend Gerald L. K. Smith. But I don't suppose you ever heard of the Proctoscopes or of Reverend Smith.

That's the brainwashing you get in those colleges. You see, the Proctoscopes tell how these big Jews got together and plotted to take over the world at a meeting they had in Russia in 1880.

No, you damned ninny. I don't think it's really that simple. When I joined the John Birch Society back in '54, two years before I saw the flying saucer that was—well, I wouldn't have seen the saucer if I hadn't read the Proctoscopes and joined the Birch Society—I *am* trying to keep it simple. I'm as sorry about those kids as anybody in town.

Murder is a messy business. I'm a lawman myself, remember.

It was Perry English, the head of the local Birch chapter, who told me about the Illuminatuses. You never heard about them neither, I reckon. Who are they? They're the gang that control the Zionists, the real hidden ones. Tibetan Nudists, Perry thinks they are, and the Zionists are just a front. So are the commies for that matter. I could tell you the real story behind rock and roll music and fluoridation and how Adam Weishaupt, the first Illuminatus, murdered George Washington and served in his place as President, establishing Illuminatus control here in America and a lot of other things you don't read in the newspapers they control. And you'd be surprised how Liz Taylor and those Bugs Bunny cartoons fit into the big picture.

There's no call to take that tone of voice. I told you I'm sorry about those kids. I'm not a maniac, you know.

Well, if you'll be quiet, then, and don't get your dandruff up. It was 23 May, back in 1956. I remember because it was my cousin Sally Lou's birthday and she was 23, too. The pair of 23s stuck in my mind. We had an anti-pornography movie at the Birch Society that night and it got me all hot and bothered, now that I recall. That was when I had the argument with Perry English. About the Illuminatuses. I told him that, seeing as they were the hidden force behind the Zionists, probably there was another hidden force behind them. That's logic, you know. But he told me I was drunk and we had words and I just stopped going to the Birch meetings after that.

You see, it was the very next day, 24 May, that I saw it.

Now, I know some of you aren't going to believe this. All those Illuminatuses in the Air Force have really done a good job on brainwashing the public about these things. But I know what I saw with my own eyes.

I was driving out to Roy Holmes's place. Nicest little spread in Mad Dog County, Roy has, and a finer man you couldn't want to meet. I had to see him about his boy, Roy Jr., who got a lot of the folks up in arms about stealing Jem Taylor's outhouse and standing it on the lawn in front of the Catholic Church where the Mexicans go. People didn't mind that so much but it was only two-three weeks since Roy Jr. had up and stole Sid Gardner's Volkswagen and put it on the roof of City Hall. They wanted the boy stopped before he committed any real mischief.

So I was driving out to see Roy Sr. and tell him he had to do something about his boy before the fool youngster got futzing around with dynamite like Pete Riley's boy that blew himself up when he was trying to convince Polly Smythe that the San Andreas Fault really extended all the way over here to West Texas. That was a sad case; the boy just wanted her to run away with him to Cuernavaca.

But there I was, fifteen miles out of town on Highway 17 as clear and dry a day as I ever saw even around these parts where most days are clear and dry. I didn't see *it* at first; I felt it. That is, the car started missing and then it stalled outright and a real queer feeling went through me, like some kind of invisible ray.

Then it was there, not more than a hundred yards above me, big as a baseball field. It was silver, mostly, but there was some kind of orange glow all around the edges. And it did look a hell of a lot like a saucer. Go ahead and laugh. Nobody can tell me what I did see and didn't see.

No, there weren't any little green men looking out of portholes at me, or anything like that. But it was there, and I felt their atomic ray or whatever it was, and my car felt it, too, because like I said the motor stalled.

Well, I just looked up and thought my time had come. Because I made the connection right away: I'd been talking about the power behind the Illuminatuses just the night before, and here they were, giving me the once-over and letting me know that you couldn't say anything without them knowing about it. And then the Voice spoke.

"Jim Carpenter," it said, "beware."

And they took off like a bat out of hell, and that was the whole experience.

Now one of the psychiatrists who tried to pump me after what happened to Suzie Belle told me that lots of people have seen flying saucers and he personally thinks there is something up there. But he said I should consider that the last part—the Voice—was my own imagination on account of I was, he says, overstimulated by the excitement of that thing coming so close. He says the voice was Auto Hypnosis.

I never heard such a damn fool thing. My car had nothing to do with it; it was stalled. And, besides, how can a car hypnotize anybody?

So there I was, forty-two years old and a full-fledged bone-fried flying-saucer contactee. Besides which, I was the only contactee who had a clear idea what those saucer people were really up to—running the Zionists and Illuminatuses and Tibetan lamas to soften us up so they could take over. I had the whole picture; but, of course, I couldn't tell anybody about it. I knew they'd clap me in the funny place if I ever breathed a word.

I never did get out to the Holmes place that day. Just went home and tied one on and thought things over. That was a shame because it was that night that Roy Jr. stole the bazooka from the Army and blew a hole big as a Greyhound bus in the high-school principal's office. Sure hated to send that boy away to the State Farm.

Well, the next ten years of my life I became what you might call a book-reading man. Fact. George Adamski visited me once and he said he never saw so many flying-saucer books in one place. Of course, he didn't take to it at all kindly when I told him that the saucerians he contacted were bare-faced liars and really plotting to enslave us. They had just brainwashed him, and he wouldn't listen to me.

No, I never saw any more saucers. Just that once as a warning.

All those years I must have been writing letters to near a thousand saucer buffs all over the country. Didn't get much help from them. They were like the Birchers: knew something was going on but didn't know what it really was. And meanwhile things were going from bad to worse all over the world and especially here in God's country. Sometimes I began to think I had a duty to speak out, to warn other folks. But my Ma didn't have any idiot children: I know when to keep my mouth shut.

My final decline and fall, as you might call it, was those damned books I mentioned earlier. *The Sensuous Man. The Sensuous Woman. The Sensuous Couple. The Sensuous Suburb.*

It was Reverend Pettigrew who complained about Floyd Gummer carrying them in his drugstore. Of course I went right down and seized them. Floyd was a good old boy and I knew he wouldn't go complaining to any American Civil Liberties Union or any of those Illuminatus-controlled eastern troublemakers. I just told him about the complaint and he handed the books over gentle as a lamb. He didn't want to be on the bad side of the Reverend any more than I did. You sure can learn more diplomacy in a small town than you can at the Paris Peace Talks.

That there is where I made my mistake, of course. Should have thrown the books in the fire right away. But no. It was in the cards, I guess. Some of us were born to hang, and even if you wear a lawman's badge for nineteen years, destiny can still ram it to you and break off the handle. Don't say any man was good or bad or lucky or unlucky until after they bury him.

I peeked into one of the books. *The Sensuous Man* I think it was. Doesn't matter: I ended up reading all four of them. Several times. Like I say, maybe I was born to be hanged.

Now I knew that things like that went on in France and in Greece. I mean I am a full-grown adult of fifty-five years of age and I know how Bob Leffert's son, young Charlie, got to be nicknamed The Sheepherder by the other boys in the high school. But this was different. It wasn't one dim-witted Charlie Leffert; it was the whole country. The Illuminatuses had succeeded in destroying our moral fibers even more completely than I'd ever imagined. Maybe it was something they put in those fluorides, but those books made me realize: that Kinsey fellow hadn't been just whistling. There really was a full-scale sexual revolution going on and I was born just one generation too soon to get in on it.

Maybe it was my age, too. A man going on sixty almost knows that he's got just so many years ahead of him.

Well, to make a long story short like they say, I drove into El Paso and bought one of those vibrators. Just kept it in the office for a while and would take it out occasionally and look at it, just thinking. I was doing a lot of thinking about those things. What I thought about the most was that one who called herself The Sensuous Woman, doing it in a tub full of jello. Every time I took a bath I'd think about that.

Suzie Belle would just never agree to that kind of foreign activities. Shoot, I could never even get her to agree to do it with the light on.

This went on for months. I'd sit there in the office looking at that vibrator and watching the high-school gals in their miniskirts going by. Seemed like they were wearing them shorter every year, despite all Reverend Pettigrew said about it in church on Sundays. There was Lem Simpson's youngest, Sally Ann, had one of those leather-type miniskirts that just came in a straight line about one-fourth inch below the Promised Land. I'd sit there and run that vibrator in my hand and watch her go by. If we only had proper censorship in this country, none of this would have happened to me. I'd just run that vibrator and think of her in a tub full of jello with me, or taking Old Faithful, you know, the French way. I'd run that vibrator like mad when I thought of that.

I tried once to reeducate Suzie Belle. Wanted her to do it in the bedroom for once instead of the bathroom. Tried to tell her it was more sophisticated and cleaner that way. She just said, "The bathroom is for dirt. The bedroom is for sleeping." I kept thinking about filling the tub with jello, but she'd think I was off my head, just like if I told her about the Voice from the flying saucer.

Being a lawman is all part of it. Folks are peaceful, mostly, in Mad Dog, but I've made my share of arrests. It would get to me sometimes, that I could just draw on any one of them when we were alone and plug him, and never anyone to doubt me if I said he drew on me first. That really got to me: how much easier it was to kill a man than to get in on all this sensuous man and sensuous woman stuff that was going on all over the country. There were days when I'd sit in the office and look at my vibrator and look at my gun and wonder.

I tried to get my mind into more wholesome channels. Started making a list of who I could be dead sure was an Illuminatus working for the saucerians. Started out with Nixon, The Muppets, Jack Warner, Charles Atlas, the Beatles, Sirhan Sirhan, and got up to about 500 names before I finally realized I couldn't be sure about anybody.

Showed that list to one of the psychiatrists afterwards. He was really impressed and said something about every mind was a treasure-house. Said I was a representative of what he called the *other* counterculture, just as isolated from the mainstream of American life as the hippies or Yippies. Guess he was right. I never did get in on all that sensuous people doings. Never did more than run that vibrator and think.

The last straw, I guess you might call it, was looking at my bank balance one day. I'm what you might call a frugal type; waste not, want not, as my Daddy always used to say. I had $18,000, and I started thinking how far that could go in a place like New York, with all those sensuous hippie girls, and how surprised they'd be to find out that an old country boy like me knows all about the chute-the-chute and the combination plate and the feathery flick and the velvet buzz saw and, hell, I got all worked up just mentioning their names.

And that was the week that Nixon was on the television from China, toasting Chairman Mao and calling Karl Marx "a great philosopher," and I could see that we was really done for. I suspect it was really Alger Hiss up there behind a rubber Nixon mask, but that doesn't make no never-mind. Why, if the mask fell off, right on TV, it wouldn't make a difference the way the moral fibers of the country are all shot to hell. People would just say, "Well, maybe the way Mr. Hiss got to be president was kinda funny, but by God now he is our president and we've got to support him." Makes no difference if it was Joe Stalin or Adolph Hitler himself for that matter. The godforsaken damned fools would just say, "He's our president and we gotta support him." That's the shape the country is in since all this pot and heroin and sex education got into the schools.

One last fling: that was all I wanted. Or one first fling. A man should have a right to one sensuous experience in his life, before the Illuminatuses and sex educators and cattle mutilators come in and establish curfews and padlock the churches and put us all in communes and start aborting our women.

It sure hurt me when I made up my mind, because after all those years I was fond of Suzie Belle. But since I turned on that vibrator and felt it purring in my hand, it had to end this way. I'd thought of myself as a good man all fifty-five years of my life, but I had to own up to the truth. The Devil was in me. I didn't want no ordinary New York girls, I wanted *New York high-school girls,* in miniskirts, just as long as they were clean and didn't use any of that dope.

Poor Suzie Belle had to die.

I spent a week researching through my old detective stories and true crime books before I hit on the perfect method. Nothing fancy—the more complicated you get, the more likely it is that you'll trip over your own feet. The best thing is something that looks like an ordinary death. You start fooling around with imaginary housebreakers and all sorts of loose ends can tangle you up. A heart attack was ideal.

Belladonna. Deadly nightshade.

The symptoms are just like a heart attack and the doc will make out the death certificate that way unless something gets his suspicions up and he does an autopsy. Well, no fear of that. Doc Hollister was a lazy old coot to start with and wouldn't want to do anything to get me riled up in the second place. And I had a gimmick to put the right idea in his head and keep it there, in the third place. And in the fourth place, he was really pretty dumb in the first place.

I didn't have any fancy notions about committing the perfect crime. None of them ever work anyhow. The real trick is to commit a convincing accident (or a realistic heart attack, like I was doing). There is no perfect murder. Once a killing is recognized as a killing, any trained investigator will get to the bottom of it in a few weeks—outside of detective stories, I mean. I wanted something that nobody would ever suspect or investigate.

On Wednesday, 23 May—I remember because it was the sixteenth anniversary of my flying saucer contact—I set my plan in motion, leaving the hen-coop door open before heading downtown to the office. Sure enough, twenty minutes later Suzie Belle was at the jail panting and gasping, complaining that the chickens was out and she couldn't catch them all herself. In a small town, things get noticed. Everybody would remember seeing her panting for breath the day before her heart attack.

I had a hell of a time catching all those chickens, by the way.

Lunchtime that day I called for Doc Hollister to go by on his way to the EAT GAS place. That's what we call it, cause it has two signs side by side, and one says EAT and the other says GAS, and it looks like it says EAT GAS when you first pass it.

Told the Doc I wanted him to come by on Saturday and check out Suzie Belle's heart on account of she was breathing hard lately.

And that was it. Everything was set. I just went on home and dropped the belladonna in her tea. She always polishes off a pot of tea by herself in the afternoon while watching *As the World Turns* and *Dark Shadows* on TV. How did I know she was going to have in all the kids from the grammar school and pour the tea into them?

Then, too, you got to remember that none of the books I read about poisons said anything about what happens when you take belladonna in subtoxic doses. None of the books said anything about the hippies taking it for kicks in New York and San Francisco. I didn't know that at all.

I had no idea what was happening when little Joe Sawyer came running up Main Street hollering that red, white, and blue cockroaches were all over him and trying to eat him.

I was running around the street trying to catch the poor boy, and he was yelling that I was a red, white, and blue cockroach, when the two Bronson girls, Sally Lou and Mary Ann, suddenly sat down in the middle of the street laughing. Old Roy Witherspoon came long in his old Ford pickup just then and has to swerve to miss them and goes right through the window of the Acme Clean While-U-Wait.

I thought the whole town was going crazy. Had no idea it was me and my deadly nightshade behind it all.

Just then the Shea boy, little Billy, gets a big crowd around him by talking about witches he can see whizzing through the air on broomsticks. They're writing in the sky, he says, like those old advertising airplanes used to do, and he's reading off what they write. Real interesting stuff it was, like "The My Lai pickle that exploded with Spider Man in sixteen Sundays a crocodile."

About then I see Paul Hurst, the middle Hurst boy, walk up to the drugstore window, make a motion like he's opening a door, and walk right through the glass. Took twenty stitches later, I heard.

It went on like that, all over town, right through the afternoon and evening. Reverend Pettigrew was telling everybody that our children had been possessed by devils, and other folks saying that it must be marijuana, and Doc Hollister explaining that it wasn't like marijuana or even LSD and he would stake his reputation that it was actually jimson weed. When he said that, I suddenly got a sinking feeling in the pit of my gut and it all began to jell for me.

The thing that hit me was that I might have turned all the poor little kids in town into dope addicts. One of the psychiatrists put my mind at ease about that later. He said a lot of hippies have tried belladonna for a trip but hardly any ever do it more than once. And it's probably not addicting, he said in a funny dry voice, because "death usually supervenes before an addictive pattern can be established." He also told me some folks in the ancient world used it in their religious rituals, and some of them never came home from church. That's how it got to be called deadly nightshade, he said.

The sun went down on a sad scene in Mad Dog that day. All the men in town were working with me, trying to catch the kids and put them in the baseball field so they couldn't run into anything hard and hurt themselves. It was hard work because those kids didn't see us or hear us. They saw and heard whatever hallucinations that belladonna gave them.

Then, just as it got dark, a whole bunch of women appeared on Main Street, carrying hunks of one of Charlie Peter's sheep that they'd caught and torn to shreds. They were chanting something that didn't make no proper sense nohow. Like "Halsy mimsy whoopsy Gort, hivey divey jivey Mort," and so on. Seems Suzie Belle had got the mothers together and poured some tea into them to calm them down.

It was a spectacle, I tell you. All those crazy women chanting about the divey jivey Mort and their fingers all red from tearing the sheep apart and the kids still running around yelling about blue pickles dancing or werewolves running across the rooftops. You couldn't tell Mad Dog from Haight Ashbury for a while there.

I can't agree at all with that one psychiatrist fellow who told me that any other place and time in history this would have been the greatest religious experience the town ever had. He said we had the Dying Asian Principal naked among us, whatever the rambling hell that means. Actually, Joe Eppert, the school principal, did help with the kids, but he kept his clothes on all the time and he ain't Asian. He's white as you or me. He's a good old boy, Joe Eppert.

The only sliver of lining to this whole cloud is that nobody actually died, although there surely were a lot of cuts and bruises and broken limbs. My lawyer tells me I'm being sued for over twenty million dollars by thirty-eight plaintiffs, besides being indicted for attempted homicide and six other offenses the prosecutor tacked on, including waging chemical warfare against the State of Texas in violation of the Geneva Conventions.

I don't mind making this statement for the US Public Health Service, and I am aware that it can be used against me at any or all of my trials. Best to make a clean breast of things when they get this bad. Suzie Belle is suing me for divorce, too, and I don't rightly blame her.

Can't nobody tell me I didn't see that flying saucer. The world is a lot weirder and more sinister than most people ever realize. You ask any of those folks who got some of that belladonna and they'd agree with me about that. Suzie Belle was still seeing a polar bear in a black turtleneck sweater following her around for two weeks afterwards. Now, I know that polar bear isn't really there, but how can anybody prove that the things we see when we're eating, say, mashed potatoes or drinking Coca-Cola, are really there. Really prove it?

Wish you could get my vibrator and send it down to the jail here. I used to get real calm and peaceful inside when I'd be running that thing and looking out at the high-school girls going by in their miniskirts. Makes me feel like a sensuous man.

Like a sophisticate.

Holy Writ

The Bible tells us to be like God, and then on page after page it describes God as a mass murderer. This may be the single most important key to the political behavior of Western Civilization.

F A S T   F O R W A R D

The coup d'etat is now the most common method of replacing governments worldwide, and has changed more administrations than all revolutions and all elections combined in the past fifteen years.

Source: *Coup D'Etat*, Edward Luttwak

CAN SUCH TECHNIQUES INDUCE BRIBE MONEY?

REV. DAVID SCOTT in tight close-up, his eyes dead-level into the camera.

SCOTT: . . . offered to turn all the records over to them. But no, that wasn't enough for those pointy-headed bureaucrats, who are trying to destroy the First Amendment as I keep telling you. Jesus knew all about them, he specifically predicted this kind of persecution, let me read it to you and see if it isn't the IRS Jesus is talking about, right here in Mark, Chapter 23 . . .

click, blurry lines

The MISSION IMPOSSIBLE crew dressed as window washers. They are washing windows on a skyscraper, tense, tight-lipped. The music is ominous.

click, blurry lines

Very serious, plump, middle-aged woman, obviously a professor. Drab background, camera hardly moves: This is Public TV.

PROFESSOR: . . . so that we never arrive at truth, but only approximate it. Each truth is partial and must be balanced by its antithesis. Right here, at this point, Hegel makes his most important contribution . . .

click, blurry lines

Very cheerful ACTRESS, exhibits orgasmic ecstasy; turns away and camera moves into tight close-up on her ass.

ACTRESS'S VOICE *(over):* . . . because they're designer jeans!

click, blurry lines

The Jumping Jesus Phenomenon

The function of This Department is to seek precise, comprehensive, synergetic, ethnomethodological, sociobiological, neurogenic, quantum-mechanical models that will prove useful to both Behaviorists and poets.

We operate here by the precisely calculated juxtaposition of idea and image, rapidly altering focus from myopia to presbytopia, looking now through the telescope and then through the microscope—as in Swift's rapid leap from Lilliput to Brobdingnag or the McLuhanesque montage of the daily newspaper. The eye skips across the headlines—BOY RAPES IRISH SETTER, PRESIDENT SAYS ECONOMY STILL TROUBLED, MAD HUNCHBACK SELLS HUNCH TO BUTCHER: FAMILY POISONED BY HUNCHBURGER, JUPITER FLY-BY FINDS BUDWEISER BEER CANS ON ASTEROID, POPE DENOUNCES STRAWBERRY DOUCHES—and if you follow a story inside you find yourself aswim in girdle advertisements.

There is one myth behind the broken words and fractured images, one metaphor that can be known by its shattered reflections, and only known by this process of shattering, because it is, given the nature of electronic speed-of-light grids, not singular but plural.

The old saying "All roads lead to Rome" registered a cybernetic fact: the Roman roads were the extended nervous system of the Empire; Rome itself was only the cortex.

The printing press exploded space-time, creating the Renaissance: a bigger nervous system, a more efficient information-processing machine.

The electronic grid is today's Appian Way, our Gutenberg Bible, our expanded-exploded in-*form*-ation system.

When you can find, just flipping the dials on your home TV, such riches as "Hegel makes his most important contribution because they're designer jeans," we are living in post-Aristotelian space-time.

Marx was wrong: Society is not determined by the means of production, but by the means of communication.

"All that is, is metaphor," as Norman O. Brown says. **The means and modes of our communicating create the society, the reality-labyrinth, in which we live.**

This necessarily implies that our psychic universe is expanding even more rapidly than the physical universe.

I have found no better way of illustrating this mental quantum-jumping than some statistics developed by French economist Georges Anderla for the Organization for Economic Cooperation and Development (OECD) in 1973.

Anderla took as his unit of measurement the known scientific facts of the year 1 A.D. For vividness, I call this unit "one jesus," using the name of the celebrated philosopher born that year. (I am here following the physical sciences where basic units are named after important individuals —e.g., the ohm, the volt, the farad, the ampere, etc.)

How long did it take to double this accumulation of knowledge, to achieve two jesuses? According to Anderla's estimates, it required 1500 years—until 1500 A.D.

Before going any further, let us ask how long it took to arrive at one jesus. One way of estimating is to take the estimated age of homo sapiens, in which case it took 40,000 to 100,000 years (depending on which estimate one accepts—i.e., how one differentiates homo sap. from his closer relatives.)

How long did it take to double again and obtain *four* jesuses? According to Anderla, it required 250 years, and we had four jesuses in our larder by 1750.

Observe the pattern thus emerging:

```
40,000 to 100,000 years  . . . .  one j
1500 years  . . . . . . . .  two j
250 years  . . . . . . . .  four j
```

Note also that, very shortly after 1750 A.D., the American Revolution occurred; the French Revolution occurred; the Mexican Revolution occurred; and all the "radical ideas" still being debated (democracy, the free market, socialism, communism, even anarchism) entered the intellectual scene. Monarchy began to collapse; the witch-hunts ended; the church declined; industrialism came to the fore. Circa 1780 both Benjamin Franklin in America and Condorcet in France proposed that science would eventually cure every disease and vanquish death—the first time in history anybody had thought of that.

Obviously, the *quadrupling* of knowledge between one A.D. and 1750 A.D. had unleashed a great deal of intellectual creativity and even some wild imagination. This seems inevitable to me. When educated persons have 100 facts for every 25 facts they had previously, they are bound to get some new ideas, too.

To continue with Georges Anderla's statistics, the next doubling took only 150 years, and by 1900 A.D. humanity had eight jesuses in our information account.

The next doubling took 50 years, and by 1950 we had 16 jesuses. (Between 1900 and 1950, there were two World Wars, fascism came and went, communism took over one-third of the world, a revolution in sexual behavior occurred according to Kinsey, the majority of intellectuals became overt atheists in the communist countries and covert atheists in the Christian countries, the age of radio drama came and went, cars replaced buggies and airplanes created "one world" travel-wise . . .)

The next doubling took *only ten years,* and by 1960 we had 32 jesuses.

A so-called Youth Revolution then occurred, happening simultaneously in all parts of the world.

The next doubling took *seven* years, and by 1967 we had 64 jesuses.

And the next doubling took six years; by 1973 (when Anderla completed his study) we have 128 jesuses.

To summarize:

40,000–100,000 years	1 j
1500 years	2 j
250 years	4 j
150 years	8 j
50 years	16 j
10 years	32 j
7 years	64 j
6 years	128 j

There is no reason to imagine that the acceleration stopped with the last estimate made by Anderla in 1973. All objective evidence (patents granted, scientific papers published, etc.) indicates that the process is continuing. Thus, we almost certainly reached 256 j around 1978–79 and will be reaching 512 j in 1982, about the time this text hits the bookstores.

In short, we are living in a mental transform space—Tielhard de Chardin's noösphere (see glossary)—that is, an omnidimensional halo expanding toward infinity in all directions.

And the electronic center of this halo of mentation, this noösphere, is potentially everywhere. It is all available to you right where you are sitting now. Just plug in a terminal. The machine doesn't care who or what you are.

F A S T   F O R W A R D

You will be able to buy a pocket computer in twelve years that outperforms the most powerful computer in the world today. It will probably cost around $200.

Source: "Thinking About the Future,"
Future Abstracts, Alexander & Alexander

NEUROSEMANTIC
KNOW-HOW QUIZ

Are the following statements true or false, or *something-else*? If *something-else*, what should we call them? Answers on page 158.

1. Water boils at 100° Centigrade.
2. PQ = QP.
3. Any set which is part of another set is smaller than the set of which it is part.
4. Raquel Welch is the most beautiful woman in the world.
5. There is a tenth planet beyond Pluto.
6. Colorless green ideas sleep furiously.
7. *Behind the Green Door* is a dirty movie.
8. The Pope is infallible in matters of faith and morals.
9. Van Gogh is a greater artist than Picasso.
10. Entropy increases in all closed systems.
11. Nothing remains of the pacing famous sea but its speech and into its talkative seven tombs the anchor dives through the floor of a church.
12. I am the Divine Effulgence of the Living God.
13. The following sentence is false.
14. The previous sentence is true.
15. All men are created equal.
16. A boy has never wept nor dashed a thousand kim.
17. All mathematics can be deduced from Set Theory.
18. My wife is the most beautiful woman in the world.

The Universe
Contains a Maybe

On March 28, 1979, something began to go wrong at the nuclear plant located at Three Mile Island in Pennsylvania. By the following morning, a Friday, it was obvious that all the people who appeared on the Tube to explain the problem were as confused and worried as any of us in the audience. Spokesmen—I didn't see a single spokesperson—from Metropolitan Edison, which owned the afflicted plant, from the Nuclear Regulatory Commission, and from the state and federal governments, all contradicted each other. If you hung by the Tube long enough, as I did, they would come back in a few hours and contradict themselves.

It was eerie for everybody, because a great horror movie called *The China Syndrome* had just opened nationwide. The trouble in the film, as at Three Mile Island, began with a malfunction in the coolant system. By Saturday morning, March 30, everybody was making nervous jokes about how far life would continue to copy art. I kept waiting for a newswoman on the scene who looked like Jane Fonda.

There was special eerieness for me, because I had spent Friday afternoon driving down the California coast—mile after mile of the incredibly beautiful seascapes of Highway One—to attend a University of California symposium on how to make the 21st century better than the 20th. The radio news bulletins from Pennsylvania began to make it seem doubtful whether there would be a 21st century.

The symposium was being held at the UC-Monterey conference center, and Monterey is another of those Spanish coastal towns so pretty and dainty that it always reminds me of Woody Allen's claim that we Californians are really living in Munchkinland. It was hard to believe, amid all those cliff-and-ocean vistas, that a world might be ending. I thought of Ezra Pound in the death-cell at Pisa, writing "Out of all this beauty something must come."

But Ezra was trying to cheer himself up, and so was I.

The conference, officially called "Transition 21: The Emerging 21st Century," began Saturday morning with a brief but touching little chat by Dr. Irving Oyle. Dr. Oyle looks and talks like your idea of an old-fashioned country doctor, and he even writes like that, as I found later when I bought two of his books. His field is what used to be called psychosomatic medicine and is now generally referred to as Holistic Health, and he believes that most of our medical problems are caused by self-punishing attitudes such as worry, anxiety, and depression. He was a great antidote to Three Mile Island, but I found his personality so engaging that I only remembered to take one note.

The note says, "Best current computer has 15 million bits, your brain 20 *billion* bits."

Dr. Oyle also said something at dinner that night which got into my notebook. He said, "Some people would worry and get depressed if you told them it was Tuesday."

What I got out of his speech and our chat at dinner was that, if there is going to be a 21st century, we'll all have to learn to be as cheerful as he is. A brain capable of handling 20 billion binary units of information should be able to solve its problems and work efficiently, once it learns to cancel self-punishing programs.

Of course, California is full of M.D.'s and psychiatrists and clinical psychologists and "Consciousness people" with the same high-energy, high-optimism glow as Dr. Oyle. That's the real reason the rest of the country, where despair is still fashionable, regards us as living in Munchkinland.

A large percentage of Californians (larger than in the rest of the country) has shared Dr. Oyle's discovery that it is both possible and desirable to operate the human brain for fun and profit without punishing programs. There's even a joke that asks how to recognize the poor people in Marin County. The answer is that they're the ones sniffing coke through food stamps. Tom Wolfe calls it the "Me Culture." Dr. Timothy Leary calls it Intelligence Intensification.

Dr. John Lilly calls it "self-metaprogramming the human biocomputer." He likes big words.

What it comes down to is the simple idea that you are in charge of organizing those 20 billion bits of information into reality tunnels that keep you, as the Consciousness Movement says, Holy-Happy-Healthy.

But what do you do when some of those bits concern a coolant failure in a nuclear plant?

The next presentation, and the best of the weekend, seemed to have the answer. This was Barbara Marx Hubbard's multimedia "Theatre of the Future," which is the greatest psychedelic high since the movie *2001.*

Hubbard is the cofounder of the Committee for the Future in Washington, DC, and one of the leading Futurists on the scene these days. She has so much bubbly optimism she almost makes Dr. Oyle look nervous by comparison. The Theatre of the Future combines slides, film, music, and Hubbard's own sexy-intellectual personality into an affirmation of humanity that might almost be the science-fiction equivalent of Beethoven's Ninth.

Except that she insists it's not science-fiction, and you tend to believe her.

"Barbara, you've got to stop talking that way," she says that anthropologist Margaret Mead once told her. "People will *stop worrying.*"

I wasn't surprised when, by the end of the weekend,

Hubbard was talking of moving to California. She really belongs out here with the other Munchkins like Tim Leary and Irving Oyle. She is terribly out of place in Washington, where worry is considered a sign of maturity and not a symptom of personal and social abuse of the brain.

Hubbard's ruling metaphor, as a literary critic might say, is the caterpillar-butterfly transformation. This is the synecdoche of evolution, to her: personal evolution, species evolution, the cosmic blueprint itself. The only reason the caterpillar "knows" how to become a butterfly, she says, is because genes contain *memory of the future.*

This is a metaphor, remember. It may be a very useful one, at that.

"To stimulate memory of the future is our purpose here," she said. The slides and the music were carrying us past O'Neill space-cities to galactic evolutionary spirals. She told us not to think of Peak Experiences as altered states of consciousness or religious transformations *only:* "**Think of your Peak Experiences as memories of the future,**" she said. Religious visionaries were the first Futurists, whether they knew it or not. The ecstatic state, she said, is a genetic foretaste of "what it will be like when humanity grows up."

Hubbard stopped the multimedia flux for a while and talked about her own intellectual development. She once read every philosopher she could find, and they disappointed her. Philosophies all tend to be nostalgic, stoic, cyclical, or existential, she said. They long for a past Golden Age, or they tell us to endure without telling us why, or they say it has all happened before and will all repeat again endlessly, or they just tell us to create our own meaning in a meaningless universe. None of them are future-oriented. None of them answers our cosmic yearning, like those religious visionaries who, in Hubbard's term, *remember the future.* I thought of Isaiah, whose words about beating swords into plowshares and studying war no more stand on the UN building as a goal to inspire us.

But religion only gives us visions; Hubbard's concern is

with the methods of achieving those visions. The Theatre of the Future swept us up into the next stages of our caterpillar-butterfly metamorphoses: Space cities . . . limitless power . . . the information explosion . . . longevity . . . higher consciousness and higher intelligence . . . "EARTHBOUND HISTORY IS OVER," Hubbard read her own words from the screen, as the music rose, "AND UNIVERSAL HISTORY HAS BEGUN."

There was a standing ovation, in which I enthusiastically joined. I haven't felt so good since the last time I heard Handel's *Messiah*.

The next speaker was Jacob Needleman, Ph.D., who was as academic and linear as Hubbard had been visionary and multimedia. He presented, again, in more documentary style, the brain/mind breakthroughs that Hubbard had more or less assumed were preparing us for new relations with space (extraterrestrial migration) and time (life extension). We are learning more and more about our own brains, he said, at the same time we are learning to use computers to extend brain power as much as all previous technology increased our muscle power.

The future of intelligence looked as good to him as it did to Hubbard.

He didn't get a standing ovation, but everybody was hungry by then.

As we went out to lunch, I heard that somebody in Pennsylvania had admitted, in front of TV cameras, that he was afraid of a *meltdown* at Three Mile Island. It didn't scare me, since I had been worried about that all along. I would have been frightened if I thought *nobody* on the scene was aware of that possibility.

Evidently, most of us ducked back to our hotel rooms during lunchbreak to check out the Tube. When we got back to the conference center, everybody had heard that people on the scene at Three Mile Island were now admitting the possibilities of both *meltdown* and *explosion*. I put it in italics because it seemed like Terry Southern was writing the script.

I still hadn't seen anyone who looked like Jane Fonda on the Tube, but otherwise, the *China Syndrome* scenario seemed to be materializing as malignantly as the mass-suicide-with-cyanide scene in *Illuminatus* had in Jonestown. Sometimes writing fiction is a creepy business. You never know what ghoulish melodrama you imagine is going to rise up, like Frankenstein's monster, and afflict you.

The first speaker after lunch was Albert Rosenfeld, whose books *The Second Genesis* and *Prolongevity* I had already read, and excellent books they are, dealing with genetic engineering, and the ongoing Biological Revolution, which he believes is going to change human life more than all the revolutions in the physical sciences since the Neolithic.

A hard-headed hard-science type I had thought him from his books: and he looked it, too, very conservatively dressed by the standards of the typical California audience before him.

Prof. Rosenfeld proceeded to blow my mind by talking about synchronicity, the weirdest idea in Jungian psychology. Maybe the *China Syndrome*/Three Mile Island coincidence had everybody thinking about synchronicity that day.

But the synchronicity that Rosenfeld mentioned was not concerned with nukes, exactly. He had found emotional meaning—synchronicity is *meaningful* coincidence, Jung says —in the fact that Anwar Sadat, Menachim Begin, and Jimmy Carter had all independently quoted Isaiah when announcing the Israeli-Egyptian peace pact.

I found it emotionally meaningful, too, since the same quote from Isaiah had been running through my head during Hubbard's presentation.

Rosenfeld went on to discuss various aspects of the biological revolution.

On the recent book *In His Image: The Cloning of a Man,* he was skeptical that it had really been done. "We'll soon be *able to do it,* if we wish," he added significantly.

On longevity, he said that he had a one-million dollar bet with a friend that they will both still be alive in a hundred years. Of course, he admitted, if he loses, his friend will find it hard to collect from his corpse.

On the misuses of genetic engineering: "A healthy person is exhilarated by the challenge of freedom," he said. And "Barbara Hubbard said most of what I want to say." People fear new technologies, he added, because they think science will be used *against* them. The right attitude toward the future was to take responsibility for it, he added.

On death and immortality: we are long past the days when Marshall Dillon looks under the cover and says, "He's dead, all right." Not in the future, but right now, Rosenfeld said, it takes a committee to decide. Medical advances continually change our definition of death and of who can be revived. There is no reason why such advances, together with longevity drugs, won't eventually culminate in physical immortality.

What the biological revolution means, he seemed to be saying, is that we, who have been the victims of evolution, are becoming its architects.

For a conservative-looking professor from Texas, who was wearing a tie even, Rosenfeld sounded a lot like a Californian. Everybody was Up when he finished. If you could bottle his mind and put it on the market, it would be the best upper since methamphetamine, without the jitters.

Then Darla Chadima, the UC organizer of the conference, got the mike and gave us the latest news from Pennsylvania. It would be about a week, she said, before it was determined if meltdown or explosion were going to happen.

She then proceeded to suggest that we, the audience, try to control the Three Mile Island plant by the *power of our minds.*

I looked around the audience with curiosity. Dr. Carl Sagan wasn't there. Nobody got up and shouted, "Bosh! Rot! Superstitious rubbish!" and stomped out. We all obediently followed Ms. Chadima in guided visualization, imagining a protective white light around the plant. We filled the white light with affirmations and good vibes. We all felt great when it was over.

Of course, I've done the White Light visualization in many Consciousness groups, and it always gets me high. There is growing scientific evidence that it works *inside* your body. Neurologists believe it releases endorphins, pain-killing compounds, from the brain, and thus tranquilizes and aids in healing.

Dr. Irving Oyle got the mike—perhaps concerned that there might be some Easterners present—and gave us several scientific or quasiscientific rationalizations about why it might work outside the body. He mentioned synchronicity. He invoked the psychons (mind-units) which some parapsychologists have posited as analogs of the photons in physics. He finally told the old joke about the man in Chicago who said "May this house be safe from tigers," every morning, and was never bothered by tigers.

In the next days, Three Mile Island gradually cooled down.

I draw no conclusions from this. Readers will divide themselves according to preference and prejudice, into those who think the light-visualization might have helped the coolant system and those who think it couldn't possibly have helped.

Next up was Dr. Brian O'Leary, the Princeton physicist and former astronaut who has been most notable lately as an advocate of space industry and space migration. Dr. O'Leary was genially amused by the White Light game, not at all offended. "California always blows my mind," he said cheerfully.

He then took us through an exciting slide show of beautiful space cities in the future, all designed by Prof. Gerard O'Neill's group at Princeton and/or the NASA-Ames group in Palo Alto, all possible with current technology, all capable of tapping enough solar power and capturing enough mineral wealth from the asteroids to end all our energy-resource worries.

Dr. O'Leary confessed to some exasperation that these esthetic space-habitats, first suggested by Prof. O'Neill in

1969 and widely publicized since 1973, are still not getting the hearing they deserve in Washington.

"Maybe evolution demands crises before each breakthrough," he said, paraphrasing part of Barbara Hubbard's presentation. He went on to consider Three Mile Island as the possible crisis that might lead us to abandon hazardous nuclear adventures and turn to O'Neill's nonpolluting and virtually limitless solar power via satellite.

O'Leary went on to discuss the differences between closed systems, where entropy must increase, and open systems, where negative entropy (or order, or information) can increase. All the gloomy prognostications around these days, he pointed out, tacitly assume a closed system, because they are Earthbound. Once you start thinking in terms of the open system made possible by space industry, solutions to all our energy and resource problems are evident.

Learning to make the conceptual jump from closed, terracentric thinking to open, outer-space thinking, O'Leary concluded, would be the Second Copernican Revolution.

He got a standing ovation, too, and richly deserved it.

And so ended Day One. We all went back to our hotel rooms and listened to more contradictory and evasive statements about Three Mile Island on the Tube. Channel 9 from San Francisco, a Public Broadcasting System station, found one expert who delighted me. He was from California governor "Jerry" Brown's energy board, and he said he didn't know what would happen at Three Mile Island. He said all the other experts were just as confused as himself, but were trying to hide it. I found his honesty refreshing.

That evening my wife Arlen and I had dinner with Barbara Hubbard, Dr. Oyle, and the other speakers. Mostly we talked about O'Leary's hope that Three Mile Island might be the crisis that would turn our society away from the nukes and toward space industry.

Hubbard said that every crisis is a potential "evolutionary driver," a stimulus to new breakthroughs. She went on to compare our present situation with that of the first vertebrates who crawled up from the sea onto the land. The whole new environment must have been a crisis to them, she argued. And, she added, there was more brain growth during that transition than at any other period of evolution.

Lyn Burwell, a columnist from a local newspaper, Russian River *Stump*, said something that impressed me even more. "The future exists first in Imagination," he said, "then in Will, then in Reality," I don't know if he intended the capitals, but I heard it that way, and it made a lot of sense to me.

The future existed already in the Imagination of those at the table. All had made the conceptual jump to what Dr. O'Leary calls the Second Copernican Revolution. With enough Will, our Imagination could become Reality. It would need a lot of moxie and political savvy, too, I thought.

Dr. David Finkelstein, the physicist, got into a rap with me about Consciousness. I was hearing everything with capitals by then. It isn't every day that you can feel yourself standing, as R. Buckminster Fuller says we all stand, between Utopia and Oblivion.

Dr. Finkelstein was intrigued by the eye-in-triangle design that I use as a motif in all my books. He said that to him the eye represented Consciousness, the triangle represented Matter, and the combination indicated that Consciousness was an emergent property of Matter.

And so, as Pepys used to write, to bed. Arlen and I tried the Tube again for a few minutes. Another expert was saying that the possibilities of meltdown or explosion were extremely slim.

He didn't say they were zero.

At breakfast Sunday morning Lyn Burwell, the columnist, told me that the nearest nuclear plant in California. Rancho Seco, had been built by Babcock and Wilcox, the same construction firm that had handled, or mishandled, the building of Three Mile Island.

On the way into the conference building, I heard that Governor Brown was considering closing Rancho Seco.

I thought of Crisis and Evolutionary Drivers.

The first speaker of the morning was Dr. Finkelstein. With his white beard and his serene manner, he reminded me of several Oriental gurus, and he started off by saying he wanted us to consider physics as a kind of poem.

He even said, unblushing, that we could consider it God's poem.

He took us then on a gentle, philosophical stroll through the more baffling enigmas, paradoxes, and mysteries of quantum mechanics. If this is God's poem, he seemed to be implying, God is a very modernistic and recondite poet. But the answer to the mysteries, he said, was to be found in jumping outside Aristotelian logic entirely.

"In addition to yes and no, there's a maybe in the universe," he said.

The maybe, he went on, is the consciousness of the observer. "Do I move my arm," he asked, "or does a law of nature move my arm? The only answer is that the I that moves my arm is a law of nature."

Quantum mechanics ceases to be mysterious, he continued, when we recognize that yes and no, space and time, even matter itself, are all epiphenomena. **What really exists, he proposed, is "a series of acts of creation," from which space, time, and matter emerge.**

Things got a bit more concrete when Finkelstein went on to talk of how much energy each new scientific paradigm allowed us to access.

Newtonian physics, he said, allowed us to use 0.0001 percent of the energy in a glass of water. I was awed, thinking that it had taken us about 30,000 years to get from the first calendar to Newton.

The chemical revolution of the 19th century, Finkelstein went on, allowed us to access 0.001 percent of the energy in the glass of water. I was awed again. It had taken only about 200 years to jump another factor of ten.

The nuclear revolution of 1945, he said, allows us to tap 1 percent of the energy in the water. I calculated quickly: only 100 years to jump again by a factor of 100. The next paradigm was due p.d.q. and should yield an energy-jump of a factor of 1,000. Could it be the open-system space industry Hubbard and O'Leary were urging? Or the consciousness revolution of Dr. Oyle, which Finkelstein also seemed to be implying? Or were both of them part of something even bigger, something that included the longevity revolution and the information revolution?

Next up was W. Brugh Joy, M.D., who gave us another dose of holistic medicine. His signal was much the same as Dr. Oyle's: the human brain is capable of functioning beautifully, joyously, ecstatically. Like any other good therapist in the country—all ten of them—he convinced you more by what he was then what he said. He was Holy-Happy-Healthy, no doubt about it.

Lunchbreak again. The news from Three Mile Island was no better, but it was no worse, either.

That afternoon, with great gusto, a Dr. Irving Kastenbaum proceeded to tear down all the hopes the previous speakers had raised. The University of California evidently felt we needed something to ground us out and bring us down after the glow of Hubbard and O'Leary and Rosenfeld and Joy. Kastenbaum thought the future would be bleak, and he didn't care much for Consciousness either. He made it sound like the worst possible predicament matter could get into.

He was an Existentialist Philosopher. His talk made me think of something Mark Twain once wrote about Italian opera. Twain said Italian opera reminded him of the night the orphanage burned down. Existentialists remind me of the year Bubonic Plague came to town.

I rode back to Berkeley with Barbara Marx Hubbard, and that cheered me up. She told me what she does when things like Three Mile Island and general human cussedness get her depressed. She meditates, she said. Then, she said, she forgets about the past and takes responsibility for the future.

It sounded like a good idea, to me.

The Three Mile Island reactor cooled down. Governor Brown did close down Rancho Seco, and eight other nuclear plants were temporarily closed down in the next month. Jane Fonda was on the Tube last night, calling upon us to close all the nukes. Everybody is saying we need a better energy source, and I think I know what it is. It's visible all day long, and it makes everything else visible to us. Brian O'Leary and his friends at Princeton have solved all the technical problems involved in bringing its energy down here.

While Jane Fonda was hollering about banning nukes last night, her message was coming to me by satellite, over Home Box Office, a cable TV system with 15 million subscribers nationally.

I don't know how many of them realize, when they turn on the Tube, that they are participating in the Space Age. But I do know a fact that large cannot excape recognition forever. Maybe, then, Three Mile Island will appear as an Evolutionary Driver, as Barbara Hubbard hopes, and solar satellites will birth space factories and space cities, and the Evolutionary Driver will carry us all the way to the stars.

Two years later, the President's Commission on the Accident at Three Mile Island issued a report saying that the problem had gotten out of control in the first three minutes, because of too many fail-safe alarms going off at once. The staff had been prepared, the Commission said, only for smaller accidents setting off fewer alarms.

During the first three minutes, over *one hundred* separate alarms had started ringing, and nobody knew which needed immediate attention. They had believed their own PR men, who claimed an accident of that magnitude was impossible.

The alarms are still going off in the heads of people who live near Three Mile Island. Psychologists continue to report post-accident emotional problems in residents of all the nearby towns.

I keep remembering Dr. Finkelstein: **"In addition to a yes and a no, the universe contains a maybe . . ."**

And a Junkyard dog is howling in the night down a windy street past the Coca-Cola advertisements and the newspapers blowing in the gutter with one headline visible: MORE WELFARE CUTS . . .

All That Is, Is Metaphor

How architecture molds our minds: The walls between urinals subliminally say that urinating is shamoful.

F A S T   F O R W A R D

By 1983, the computer industry will probably be the number one money-making industry in the world.

Source: *The Micro Millenium,* Chris Evans

There's A Handcuff On Them:
A CONVERSATION WITH
ROBERT ANTON WILSON

Why arc you writing twelve novels about a subject as bizarre as the alleged Illuminati, a conspiracy which is only taken seriously by extreme right-wing cranks?

There are some left-wingers who believe in the Illuminati, too, and there is a paradox there—an identity of opposites—that I find amusing and intriguing. Also, many sober and scholarly radicals believe in something which, although not called the Illuminati, acts in many respects like part of the Illuminati. I refer to the Power Elite of sociologist C. Wright Mills, the Yankee Establishment of historian Carl Oglesby, the Military-Industrial Complex, etc.

What is even more enigmatic, and therefore exciting to me as a writer of fable and satire, is that there are brigades of people who believe in the Illuminati but do not regard them as malign or malicious. I refer to the occultists of a dozen traditions who believe the Illuminati (or the Great White Brotherhood, or the Secret Chiefs, or the Nine Unknown) are the protectors or custodians of this planet. There is a double ambiguity here—do the esoteric Illuminated Ones really exist? and are they the Good Guys or the Bad Guys?—that seems to me the artistic synecdoche for the perplexities of our age. Within this ambiguity lurk deep mythological, psychological, and neuropolitical tensions which are irresistibly comic (and horrific) to me as a social satirist and psychohistorian.

What about the debate as to whether the *Illuminatus!* books are really science fiction or not? How do you stand on that?

I regard them as guerilla ontology. They include, but are not limited to, the traditional perimeter of science fiction. In mainstream science fiction you can slip in a mystical or occult idea only by first rationalizing it with a pseudoscientific explanation. I drop them in without rationalizing them, to suggest that the scientific framework itself may be inadequate. Then, at other points, I will rationalize, in the most materialistic and "reductionist" manner, just to give a hotfoot to the mystics. I am frankly out to scare the bejesus out of my readers at times, and at other times I raise Utopian hopes and cosmic vistas that only the most far-out Futurists dare to espouse these days. At some point, with one version or another of the Illuminati mythos, I hope to touch on every reader's deepest hopes and anxieties. By this continuous refocusing without ever committing myself to one view, I think I have found what hundreds of writers have sought: a way to force the reader to think for himself or herself. I even take some gratification from the fact that the only hostile reviews the books have received so far (three of them) all said they found the saga so awful that they didn't read more than 50 pages of the first novel. I was amused that they all stopped at the same point. I assume, immodestly, that thinking was such an unfamiliar chore to these reviewers that they found it painful. The question implicit on every page of the series—Is this real or a put-on?—seems cute and trivial only until a live nerve of your own fears and hopes is touched.

You constantly toy with the notion that the Illuminati might be extraterrestrials. How serious are you about that?

I'm at least as serious as Dr. John Lilly, who has written extensively about his possible contacts (he never says they're really real) with higher intelligences from elsewhere in space-time. It is the best-kept secret of our age that literally dozens of other scientists working in the areas of consciousness research, UFOlogy, and the paranormal have had experiences similar to Lilly's, although most of them refuse to talk about this in public. One who does talk, a bit too wildly for my taste, is Dr. Andrija Puharich, who believes literally in the Hoovans (benign extraterrestrials) allegedly communicating through Uri Geller. It is easy to laugh at Dr. Puharich, but a look at his long list of scientific achievements shows that he is no fool. He has merely been through what most of the characters in my Illuminati books go through: experiences so mind-boggling that they demand an extravagant explanation. This area is perfect for my brand of guerilla ontology, since you can always get a startlingly different overview just by tilting your perspective slightly. Some revisionist UFOlogists, for instance, believe the whole UFO phenomenon is being produced by surviving Nazis: the UFO, they say, was Hitler's last secret weapon. Without going that far, Dr. Jacques Vallée, an astronomer and computer scientist, makes a damned good case that the phenomenon is the work of *some* quite terrestrial Intelligence Agency endeavoring to alter consciousness and behavior—emic realities (see glossary in text)—on a worldwide scale. If this is true, something very much like the mind-warping Illuminati feared by the most rabid paranoids really exists, whether it calls itself the Illuminati or not.

Very concretely, what aspect of the Illuminati mythos do you come closest to taking seriously?

Very concretely, the psychedelic brainwashing scenes in *The Eye in the Pyramid* were written to demonstrate the techniques by which perceived (emic) realities can be drastically altered. As an expert in guerilla ontology, I realized back in '69, when those scenes were conceived, that there are also experts in guerilla neurology, and that many of them do not have my ethical squeamishness. I take the subsequent revelations about the CIA's MK-ULTRA and LSD programs as documentation of my thesis.

Similarly, in *The Golden Apple*, my collaborator, Bob Shea, wrote a scene in which several thousand Nazi soldiers are mind-programmed to commit mass suicide with cyanide. I take the Jonestown tragedy as further confirmation that we weren't drilling in a dry hole. Being interested in Jung's notion of synchronicity (meaningful coincidence), I am impressed by the facts that our Jonestown zombies used the same poison, cyanide, as the Nazis in our novel, and that they held their own Götterdämmerung during the first American stage production of *Illuminatus!* in Seattle. I went up to Seattle to see the show, and it was eerie to hear those lines about mass suicide with cyanide while the newspapers were full of the grisly details. Our science fiction had become fact in only ten years.

In my more conceited moments I even think that the unjust and neurologically naive verdict in the Patty Hearst case would have been prevented if the jury had read and understood the *Illuminatus!* novels. But so many people regard the whole series as *merely* satire that I now find myself, like Bernard Shaw, forced to repeat over and over that the biggest joke is that I am completely serious.

You have also coauthored a book with Dr. Timothy Leary called *Neuropolitics*. Does that relate to your preoccupation with mind manipulation?

You betta you ass. The parts of *Neuropolitics* in which I acted as collaborator deal entirely with mindwashing and brain programming. Every tribe and nation has its own neurological style, its way of orchestrating the received signals into emic Gestalts (local reality-tunnels). Every infant quickly learns a few crude power tactics and emotional games or cons to impose one's own reality on others. Politicians, clergymen, and advertisers become pragmatic experts at such reality brokering. Scientific understanding of these processes is de facto producing an Illuminati, or several rival bands of them, brain-change experts who are out to program you and me into their favorite reality-labyrinths.

These Orwellian reflections are, of course, only one side of the coin. (Here's where guerilla ontology tilts the perspective again.) Neurological politics raises the possibility of what I call the HEAD Revolution: Hedonic Engineering And Development. Anyone who learns how to push his or her own buttons, debug old and obsolete programs, reprogram and metaprogram his or her own imprinted and conditioned circuitry, can then make a quantum jump in neural efficiency. Higher intelligence, greater emotional equilibrium, acceleration of change and growth, intensification of experienced time, are just some of the amusing and instructive programs possible. We can all learn to use our brains for fun and profit. In that case, we can all become members of the Illuminati—self-programmers, co-creators of our own reality.

How has the *Illuminatus!* series affected your own life?

The longer I work on the series, the weirder and funnier my mail gets, for one thing. Mae Brussell, the queen of conspiracy buffs, has charged in *Conspiracy Digest* that I am an agent of the Rockefeller (Yankee) cabal. I solemnly confessed in the next issue, adding "Woof! Woof! Woof!" to confuse matters. I am sure some readers are still trying to decode the extraterrestrial signal in those mysterious words. A chap in Canada, doing a survey of occult groups, forwarded a form questionnaire on which he had typed one extra question just for me: "Would you comment on the rumor that you are the head of the Illuminati?" I replied, "A toenail at most."

As an experiment, I once wrote to several occult magazines, mentioning in passing—casually, you know—that I *am* the head of the Illuminati. The first four responses were from gents who also claimed to be the head of the Illuminati; but since they accepted me as the head, too, I gather they were all guerilla ontologists like me. The fifth also claimed to be the real head of the Illuminati and threatened to sue me, although he neglected to make clear what he was going to sue me for. I replied with a form I use for such occasions, saying that his letter would not program into my computer and asking him to resubmit it in Basic. I haven't heard from him since.

On the other hand, I could tell you a few stories that would make the Close Encounters of Dr. Lilly or even Dr. Puharich seem tame by comparison. Some of the people, or humanoids, I've encountered since starting this game have left behind mysteries that still have me perplexed. I remain cheerfully agnostic. After all, the real question posed in the *Illuminatus!* books is: **if your reality-labyrinth is not created by your brain, as suggested above, who or what is creating it?** And if the control buttons are outside you, should not your principal concern be with recapturing the Reality Studio and taking charge of your own script?

F A S T   F O R W A R D

Alexander Ostrowski is believed to be the last man to know every branch of mathematics ca. 1915. In the late 1940s, John Von Neumann estimated that the best-informed mathematicians of the time probably knew about 10 percent of the then-published papers and theorems. In the 1960s, Stanley Ulam estimated that 200,000 new theorems were being published every year. Today, there are 3,000 branches of mathematical knowledge, and hardly any mathematician is expert in more than two or three of them: more than 99 percent of math is unknown to any individual mathematician.

Source: *The Mathematical Experience*, P. J. Davis and R. Hersh

Tactical Thought

If I were the head of the Illuminati, I certainly would not call it by that name; I'd call it something innocuous, like the Parent-Teachers Association. Better still, I'd call it the John Birch Society, and advertise it as an organization *opposed* to the Illuminati. That way I'd be able to rope in all the people who are against the Illuminati and use them as unwitting dupes.

This is such a plausible idea that if the Illuminati do exist, they must have thought of it already.

F A S T   F O R W A R D

Circa 1900, about 4 percent of the population of the US had attended college. Circa 1970, it was 40 percent.

Source: *The Pound Era*, Hugh Kenner

From The Universe Next Store:
MITCHELL BROTHERS
RAIDED AGAIN

Police raided the Mitchell Brothers adult theatre in San Francisco again today and arrested three performers for making lewd and perverted noises.

Mayor Diane Feinstein, in a press conference, congratulated the police for their vigilance and said, "This administration intends to wipe out that kind of smut completely. I believe in the First Amendment, but there is no room for mere filth in our city."

Arresting officer Sgt. Joe Friday told reporters that when he entered the theatre one of the performers was playing Beethoven's Waldstein Sonata on a p——o.

"It was very passionate," Sgt. Friday said, "and I could see that people in the audience were kind of glazed-over and some of them seemed to be real degenerates and were breathing hard and moving their hands in time to the noise."

Two other performers were also taken into custody for allegedly rendering Vivaldi's "Concerto for H——p and O——e."

Attorney Hagbard Celine of the Unistat Civil Liberties Union has denounced the police. "They should be out stopping violent crimes," Celine told reporters. "After all, if people want to hear that particular kind of noises, well, you or I might not like it, but if they're not harming anybody, the government has no business harassing them."

District Attorney Arlo Smith denounced Celine's arguments as "spurious."

"That kind of noise is just plain filth," Smith snapped angrily, "and everybody knows it."

Smith added, "Our society is based on the integrity of the family. To talk of this as a 'victimless crime' is nonsense.

People come out of the theatre, after hearing those sensual and emotional noises, and they're just not in their right minds."

Justin Case of the Aural Freedom League announced that his group will pay the legal fees of the Mitchell Brothers Theatre in this case.

"Such persecutions should have ended in the Dark Ages," Case told reporters. "There is no such thing as immoral harmony. Why, some noises can be beautiful, spiritual experiences, just like painting or fucking."

Case's group has been arrested several times for staging "Aural Freedom" protests at which voluptuous noises were made with h——s and s——g instruments.

THE JUNKYARD DOG

I don't say this to my people. They'd think I'm nuts. I think they [the CIA] killed Dorothy Hunt.

Charles Colson
Time, *July 8, 1974*

Many passages in my novels were produced by the cut-up method invented by William S. Burroughs and Brion Gysin. I was sneaky about it; the cut-ups were inserted where my characters were dreaming or on drugs, and I did not explicitly tell the reader that this prose was produced by *mechanical techniques.*

Scientists are allowed to experiment, and engineers may use machine-age industrial processes, but writers are supposed to remain in the pre-Einsteinian murk. Movie directors use montage, and painters use collage, but we writers are still expected to pretend that the linear mode is ordained by God or too sacred to be breached. The exact reasons why literature should remain stuck in the early 19th century while the rest of our culture is moving rapidly toward the 21st are, to say the least of it, obscure to me.

The cut-up method is both random and stochastic; it disconnects linguistic tropisms and reconnects on a higher, or more subtle, level of coherence. You take a page you've just written and cut it into four quarters. Shuffle them and type up the results. Throw away what you don't like. Then take two pages and quarter each of them. Good. Now you have eight pieces to shuffle. Take somebody else's prose or poetry and add that to the stew. Always edit, to keep only the wild green lines.

You can have lots of fun deciding how to punctuate. You can put it into paragraphs, or into a simulation of dialogue, or make it look like somebody's internal stream-of-consciousness. You can even mix it with other elements from pieces that haven't been cut up and permutated. *F A S T F O R W A R D:* On December 8, 1972, United Airlines Flight 553 left Washington and headed for Chicago. On board was Dorothy Hunt, wife of Watergate conspirator E. Howard Hunt, carrying an unknown sum of bribe money from the White House. A mile and a half short of Chicago's Midway Airport, Flight 553 crashed, killing everybody aboard.

The Junkyard Dog is a repeating tape loop creating the thoughts, feelings and (apparent) sense impressions of the Cowboy Elite.

You can mix anything in. Take some bit of prose that strikes you as particularly pompous and obtuse, cut it up, and the results can be quite amusing:

"Somehow it just doesn't caricature—"

"Negativism Himself?"

"Such ranting and raving books . . ."

"Wasting his time repeating a half step back."

"Anti-environmentalist plot . . . that is too close . . ."

Now that's a typical ass-hole reviewer talking to himself. Add some Arthur Flegenheimer to the brew and it gets wilder and funnier:

"You got no trigger but somehow it just doesn't get ahead," the psychiatrist commented.

"There are many funny prejudices . . . Hobo and Pobo I think . . . a better future is jumping around . . ." Sheriff Carpenter explained.

"Reserve decision . . . police, police . . . dog biscuit is too close. . ." one of the kids on belladonna moaned happily.

District Attorney Arlo Smith is today's Appian Way, our Gutenberg Bible: we are living in linguistic tropisms.

You can have lots of fun in the sexual attitudes of the parents . . . Simon Moon peers to some unknown destination . . . No more muddy juxtaposition :

"Pope denounces one jesus . . ." Blake Williams muttered. "How long did it take by *mechanical techniques?*"

Very few physicists can certainly reach down and stop the Russian calamity—it's no problem for the reality-labyrinth in which we live—Not singular but plural, crying for peace— Please advise—

"Wheeler had another mammalian behavior, as Kinsey said . . ." The voice was indistinct, buzzing.

"Different maps for making lewd and perverted noises . . ."

"It was very passionate . . . right here in Mark, Chapter 23 . . ." Sheriff Carpenter was looking worried by now.

Each truth is partial and must be balanced on her ass.

On April 23, 1014, Brian Boru pushed open the door of M.M.M. "Mystical Books of All Ages" and passed through the possibility of *meltdown.*

This sixfold synergy explains why feral children are not "fully human." A human is part of a *plural system* of human relations. The feral child has never been humanized; and conversely, humanized persons in isolation for long times find the plural human system collapsing upon them. They enter trans-human or at least transpersonal reality-tunnels. This is the mystical bliss-out of shipwrecked sailors and of John Lilly in his Samadhi-tank.

"Richardson has no known connection with Hinkley but the Junkyard Dog and by the end of it I was having acute anxiety . . ."

Energy in-forms matter, as I in-form you when I talk to you. Thus, Claude Shannon's theory of information (in-form-ation) applies to all systems: That which is measured is in-formed, *tuned-in.*

We have come to bring you MORE WELFARE CUTS.

If you've never had an orgasm, you've never had *orgas-matron* . . . to give a hot-foot to the renewables . . . no mustache—Perhaps a century from now Greenspun becomes a functional cosmos syndicate.

A Revolutionary New Concept in Art Machines . . . Over 24 different selections to choose from! Guilt . . . money . . . despair . . . Alien signals . . . "A 4000-mile *cunt*? That'a a very funny metaphor, Professor" . . . existential and conceptual . . .

At last! An Art Machine that really works designed for you and yours by the Bureau of Common Sense

Any set which is part of another set of whom the Rockefellers are symbols . . . John Fitzgerald Kennedy who was ON ASTEROID . . . There is one myth behind chimney sweeps . . . Hiroshima—growing awareness of the possibility of nuclear holocaust—Damn it, the flying saucer *is* connected—*mean as a cyanide vibrator* . . .

Some of these bits concern a third and superior mind: that is doing what people say you cannot do.

"The West Point Class of 1915 will destroy Associated Press and literature," Sheriff Carpenter warned grimly.

"Consciousness is information received and decoded by the executive organ of this social influence. The Empire never ended."

"*Skeletons* in the sexual attitudes of the parents!"

Simon Moon peers unbelievingly at the course titles offered by Dr. Error's House of Mystery:

MENTAL PATIENTS LIBERATION
VEGETARIANISM AND WORLD HUNGER
HOW TO COPE WITH MARXIST FREAKS
ANARCHY AND FEMINISM
LEARNING RELIGION STRAIGHT FROM GOD

As Philip K. Dick says in *Valis*, "We did not fall because of moral error; we fell because of intellectual error: that of taking the phenomenal world as real."

The Empire, of course, insists on imprinting its own repeating tape loops on your brain. These loops, defining "you" and the "external world" in one way only, make up the official reality-labyrinth that you encounter everywhere. **You encounter it everywhere because you carry it with you, in your**

brain. These loops are the 'mind-forg'd manacles" that Blake warned us about 200 years ago.

"They won't let me get up. Give me something."

"Babylonian astrology is also known as the box or the cage or Euclidean space."

"Then I couldn't find the Old Testament God . . ."

"A chicken in the Vatican by 1990!"

"My leaves have drifted. Pull me out."

Shakespeare's favorite metaphor was the *garden*. Gentle Will brings flowers with him wherever he goes: the court of Denmark, ancient Rome, Prospero's island.

"The contact has been made . . . minds enflamed . . ."

Just enough of each dirty secret was revealed to discredit Nixon; no dirty secret was pursued to its full ramifications. An Iron Curtain dropped, we suddenly had a new President (who immediately pardoned Nixon) and Watergate was all over, a part of history with Waterloo and the Battle of Clontarf. **"The Empire never ended."**

"What you don't like . . . somebody else's prose blowing in the streets," Joyce commented ironically.

"We are morally innocent; it is the Empire . . ."

There is very little information in a political speech, because you always know what is coming next. A great poem, on the other hand, is information-rich in Weiner's sense.

As Phil Dick says, again in *Valis,* "The Empire is the institution, the codification, of derangement; it is insane and imposes its insanity on us by violence, because its nature is a violent one."

Before going any further let us ask the Mick Jagger of 2005:

"Why not? Any guy today predicts a swing back. I saw myself out there surrounded by conspiracies. A so-called youth revolution had eight jesuses. Real Capital is produced rapidly increasing maternal behavior."

The speed of travel has increased, ignoring the gate in time.

Pisa, in the 23rd year of Marilyn Chambers . . .

David A. Stockman sums up the Reagan Administration's philosophy in two pithy aphorisms: "Nobody is entitled to anything" and "We want a budget director who is mean as a Junkyard Dog." Got it?

"The father and the mother are the probability of project success . . . Colorless green junkyard minimizes the cost and time required . . ."

Contact has been made.

The Persecution and Assassination of the Parapsychologists as Performed by the Inmates of the American Association for the Advancement of Science under the Direction of the Amazing Randi

The Novelist was working on a huge, Cyclopean sword-and-sorcery epic set in 18th-century Europe, full of duels and seductions and revolutions and a cast that included such egregious gentry as Napoleon and the Marquis de Sade. It promised to be a rather juicy bit of work; and then *High Times* called and asked if he would attend the 1980 San Francisco meeting of the American Association for the Advancement of Science and write an article about it.

"Ah, time! cash! art! and patience!" as Herman Melville once moaned. Ah, cash, especially.

The Novelist was not at all sure he wanted to be dragged out of the Novel while it was going well. But *High Times* hooked him, not just with $$$$ but with the proposal that they wanted him to observe how the parapsychologists were handled, or manhandled, this time around.

You see, at the last AAAS meeting, in Houston in 1979, Dr. John Archibald Wheeler, who is to physics what Paul McCartney is to Rock, had damned and blasted the parapsychologists from here to Hell and back. Dr. Wheeler is a real Heavy; his contributions to quantum theory, gravitational geometry and other arcane branches of physics are literally cosmic in import. He also has the distinction of sometimes being called the Father of the Hydrogen Bomb, except in those circles where Dr. Edward Teller is called the Father of the Hydrogen Bomb; why anybody would claim paternity in such a case is a mystery to the uninitiate. The Novelist would personally rather be dubbed the Father of the Bubonic Plague; but, you know, different strokes for different folks; different scenes for different genes, etc.

Wheeler has another distinction, for which the Novelist loves him dearly. In a weak moment, or a whimsical moment, or maybe after sniffing too much glue while pasting up his press clippings, Wheeler put his name on a paper with two other physicists named Everett and Graham, in which they proposed that everything that can happen, in effect, does happen; that there are literally millions of millions of millions of universes, each as vast in space and time as this one, in which slightly distorted xerox copies of each of us are going through variations of the life-scripts we are going through here.

Concretely, that seems to mean that in the universe next door, Dr. Wheeler never put his name on such a bizarre speculation; and in the universe two jumps away, he never became a physicist at all, but is a ballet dancer perhaps; and further over he was never born because his mother had an abortion or never met his father; and so on, and on, through all possible permutations.

If this makes you dizzy, take comfort in the thought that it only includes *possible* universes. The Everett-Wheeler-Graham Model, or EWG as it's called for short, does not say that copies of you are wandering around in totally impossible universes.

Very few physicists take this model seriously (and it is rumored that they are all acid-heads) but the Novelist loves it because, as literature, it's superb.

And yet, in 1979, Dr. Wheeler, the man who loaned his prestigious name to this enormous *katzenjammer*, denounced the parapsychologists for being weird. It was like Salvador Dali complaining Picasso wasn't realistic.

Well, it just goes to show, as said before: different lanes for different brains, different models for different muddles.

But Dr. Wheeler had not just fulminated against the parapsychologists in Houston; he had gone a lot further, saying they should be kicked the hell out of the American Association for the Advancement of Science for their sloppy research techniques. "Sloppy research technique" is what a scientist calls it when another scientist gets lab results he dislikes.

This had led to a lot of subsequent debate in *Science*, the journal of the AAAS. Another physicist, who shall be nameless, had characterized the intellectual level of that debate, for the Novelist, by saying the typical communique sounded like, "Dear Sirs: I did *not* call my learned colleague an ass. I called him an imbecile."

Scientists, like lesser mortals, tend to fall in love with their own ideas, and sometimes get territorial and protective about them. We are a domesticated primate species, after all.

The Novelist actually had his own private reasons for wanting to check out how parapsychologists, and other heretics, were treated at the 1980 AAAS National Meeting. He had no high regard for parapsychologists himself; they seemed to him to lack imagination, poetry, and whimsey—he thought they should all expand their consciousness by studying modern physics. But he was interested in heretics in general and how the scientific Establishment treats them.

This interest was particularly concrete at this time because there was one part of the historical Novel that was giving him trouble. His hero, Sigismundo Celine, had seen a meteorite fall. Celine had dragged the Damned Thing, which couldn't exist according to 18th-century science, to the Academy of Sciences in Paris. Naturally, he was roundly denounced and mocked for his troubles. This was accurate: anybody who reported a meteorite to 18th-century scientists was treated like a Close Encounterer of the Third Kind today.

The problem was in recreating the mental set of the scientists of 1780, those self-declared Men of Reason who were so sure of their own enlightenment. Certainly they would not reject Celine's meteorite with the same arguments used by the Holy Inquisition to refute what Galileo saw through his telescope—"It's not in the Bible or Aristotle, so it can't be true." And yet they did reject all evidence of meteorites.

How did they convince themselves of their own rationality while refusing to look at the actual facts about meteorites?

The Novelist decided that checking out how the Triple-A-S deals with unorthodoxy today would give him some insight into how the Academy of Sciences dealt with meteorites in 1780.

And so, undergoing a topological transformation, the Novelist-turned-Journalist arrived at the San Francisco Hilton the second day of the AAAS meeting to drink impressions, and hopefully some wisdom, from a panel on "Science and Pseudoscience."

The Journalist had a pretty good idea of what "pseudoscience" means. People who had been reporting the current equivalent of meteorites were going to be dumped on; that's what it means. It was an axiom of his philosophy that *ten thousand* trained witnesses reporting something which doesn't fit the local emic tunnel-reality have less credibility than *two* drunken participants in an auto accident.

You can already see that the Journalist had his mind poisoned by the pernicious idea that he was going to witness a kind of heresy trial of those who, because of dope, delusions or (maybe!) clearer-than-average vision, were seeing things the AAAS doesn't want to hear about. You might say that was a paranoid head-set, or that it was based on a cynical view of how domesticated primates behave when they get together in groups to define Truth, but at least the Journalist is upfront with himself and his readers about his own Heresies.

Naturally, the symposium on Damnable Blasphemers and How to Get Rid of Them—I mean, the panel on "Science and Pseudoscience"—was 'not held at the time and place announced on the schedule. That's another thing about domesticated primates when they get together in groups: They never do things when they say they will. It's one of Parkinson's Laws. Parkinson was one of the Journalist's favorite scientists because everybody said that what Parkinson wrote was satire disguised as science. The Journalist was more than half convinced that the only way to publish truth among domesticated primates was to let them think it was satire.

So, after going back to the Press Room and finding the new date and time for the Heresy Trial, the Journalist went and sat in on a press conference being held by ecologist Barry Commoner. Dr. Commoner, he found, is just as handsome as his photographs and looks exactly like everybody's idea of a Distinguished Elderly Scientist. If that wasn't his profession already, Dr. Commoner could have a great career in Hollywood playing Distinguished Elderly Scientists in films. No wonder he's running for President.

Dr. Commoner said that we're running out of **non-renewable** resources but that there are plenty of **renewable** resources available to us. The only problem we have, he said, is that the people who run our society don't seem to want to convert from non-renewables to renewables.

We only have five to ten years in which to begin retooling for renewables, Dr. Commoner went on. He explained the law of supply and demand to us. **As the non-renewables run out, he said, their cost will go up, and up, and up, because it will be harder to find them.**

The Journalist tried to imagine Exxon getting out of non-renewable oil (with the profits there going up, and up, and up . . .) into renewable solar energy (with the profit picture there entirely unclear at this point). Obviously, the only way Exxon will do it is if the President sends the Army, the Navy, the Marines and the Air Force to make them do it.

It became clear that Dr. Commoner is not running for President just because he looked in the mirror one morning and realized that he looks like a President should look.

The Journalist, turning back into the Novelist, imagined Dr. Commoner trying to persuade the Board of Directors of Exxon that they should, for the good of humanity, switch from oil to solar. It would be like the opening scenes of *2001,* he decided. The alpha male would swell his muscles and roar; the other primates would take the signal and swell their muscles and roar; then they would show Dr. Commoner the door to the street.

"Do not meddle in the affairs of primates, for they are subtle and quick to anger," as the *Galactic Guide to Primitive Planets* says.

It seemed likely to the Journalist that the real reason Dr. Commoner wants to be President is so that when Exxon swells up and barks at him, he can swell the federal bureaucracy and bark back at them, louder. Normal mammalian behavior, as Kinsey said in a different context.

And there was more zoological interest (thought the Journalist, rapidly turning into a Sociobiologist) when the great pseudoscience panel finally did convene the following morning. There were five speakers but only one viewpoint. If the "pseudoscientists" are those who think they have found meteorites, here was a debate on the issue by five men who knew damned well that there were no meteorites.

This was hardly astonishing to the Sociobiologist. He remembered the debate on Dr. Immanuel Velikovsky's comet heresies staged by TV scientist Carl Sagan at the AAAS meeting in 1971, where the panel consisted of Sagan, two other opponents of Velikovsky, and poor old Velikovsky himself. That three-to-one edge led to a certain amount of bad temper, since it made Velikovsky feel Sagan's gang were mobbing him. There would be no such uncouthness in this panel, however, since it was 5-to-0 instead of 3-to-1. You can't beat that for couthness.

Out of a desire to demonstrate the spirit of fair play and free enquiry, however, the heretics were allowed into the audience, where they promptly clustered themselves up front directly under the panelists in what the Journalist quickly described to himself as "the sinner's bench." To the Sociobiologist, it illustrated what Tim Leary calls the vertical polarity of the emotional-territorial circuit: any primate group defines authority in terms of who is *higher* and who is *lower*.

(That's why dictators like to talk from balconies, Leary says.) So the primates on the stage were the Authorities here, and the heretics *down* on the sinner's bench had to look *up* at them all morning long.

Of course, the heretics were not gagged or tied to their chairs; this wasn't a Chicago courtroom, thank God, but a learned group of sages. The heretics were actually allowed five minutes each to defend themselves, later on, after the panel had three hours to denounce them in advance, and after most of the audience had left.

That's certainly fair, or some approximation of fairness, even if it doesn't quite satisfy the FCC's equal-time doctrine.

The first speaker was Dr. Rolf Sinclair of the National Science Federation. He said a lot of nice things about science, which was not surprising; if the first speaker had been the Pope, one would have expected him to say a lot of nice things about religion.

The Journalist took only one note during this sermonette. It said "Scientists intensively competitive." Memory (always less reliable than the trusty notebook) indicates that Sinclair thought it was good that scientists are competitive, but whether this was on Darwinian or Republican grounds is not clear.

One did get the impression, however, that Sinclair was trying very hard to be decent to everybody, including the heretics in the sinner's bench.

The next speaker was livelier. This was Dr. Ray Hyman of the University of Oregon. He defined "pseudoscience" rather circularly as "pathological science" and then defined that as "the science of things that aren't so." One began to feel that Lemuel Gulliver should have been reporting this discourse. "The first Rule among these Learn'd Persons," Gulliver might write, "is that Heresy is False, and that Falsity is Untrue, and that, furthermore, the Untrue is Heretical."

"But," Gulliver's host (who looks like a horse and talks like G. I. Gurdjieff) might press, "how do they Determine what is Heretical and False and Untrue?"

"They have an Infallible Method," Gulliver would reply, "which is This: They only Believe that which can be Demonstrated to their Reason, and they are able to Demonstrate to their Reason only those Propositions which they are willing to Believe."

But at this point it was obvious that the Journalist was goofing off and the Novelist had seized the chance to take over the assignment. The Journalist resumed control, and Dr. Hyman, not being a character in a satirical novel but a real live *mensch*, then surprised both of us by arguing, rather somberly, that the pathology in "pathological science" was not just in the heretics but in the scientific Establishment itself.

What makes for pathology, Hyman said, beginning to sound like Gregory Bateson, is a jamming or warping in the communication process. Those who tried to prevent the publication of Dr. Velikovsky's cosmic catastrophe books back in the 1950s, he said, created more pathology than Velikovsky's theories ever could.

The way to determine truth, Hyman went on vigorously, is to allow all viewpoints to be discussed.

This was such a radical notion, in these surroundings, that the Sociobiologist expected Hyman to be ejected from the *alpha males* up on the stage and sent to sit among the heretics in the sinner's bench. But Hyman made a nice recovery, rushing on to heap ridicule on the ideas of teleportation and "psychic force" (two of the most Damnable of all Heresies, according to the Establishment). He was on the Right Side after all, and only the most Agnewesque Establishmentarians would accuse him of being "squishy-soft" on heresy for believing in debate.

That "psychic force" business is especially irritating to the Establishment because, no matter how many times they condemn it as false, it keeps getting rediscovered, or rehallucinated, by otherwise sober people. Dr. Stanley Krippner, former president of the Association for Humanistic Psychology and a leading candidate for King of the Heretics, if such an anarchistic group had a King, lists over ninety cases of the rediscovery, or rehallucination, of this psychic force in the history of science. For instance, the alchemist Ibn Sina discovered or hallucinated it in the 12th century and called it Anima Mundi. Paracelsus discovered-or-hallucinated it as Munia in the 16th century; Luigi Galvani, the electrical pioneer, called it Life Force in 1790; Johann von Goethe named it *Gestaltung* in 1800; Baron Karl von Reichenbach dubbed it the Odic Force in the mid-19th century, and used it to cure diseases; and so on, and so on.

Indeed, the more the idea gets condemned, the more people who seem to feel the force is with them. Rudolph Steiner called it the Etheric Force in 1900; William McDougall, the Hormic Energy, 1920; Henri Bergson, *élan vital,* also 1920; Alexander Gurwitsch, the mitogenetic ray, 1937; Wilhelm Reich, orgone, 1937; V. S. Grischenko, bioplasma, 1944; Henry Margenau, quasi-electrostatic field, 1959; Andrija Puharich, psi plasma, 1962; Charles Musés, noetic energy, 1972; and on, and on. Sure is a lot of hallucination going on among the heretics.

Dopers *all* seem to have this hallucination; they call the Force simply "the vibes," subdivided into "good vibes" and "bad vibes." Shows what Permanent Brain Damage will do.

And this brings up another thought to the Historian, who pushes the Journalist aside for a moment. Hyman, in speaking of the infestation of the Establishment itself by "pathology," mentioned the attempt to suppress Velikovsky's books in the 1950s. It is moderately curious that he should choose that example—an *attempt* to suppress books—when something far more pathological, from a civil libertarian point of view, occurred in the 1950s. For it was in 1957 that an actual suppression, not an attempted suppression, occurred. when the Feds, egged on by the American Medical Association, seized all the books of Dr. Wilhelm Reich, 30 years of scientific research, and burned them in an incinerator in New York City. **No: that is not a misprint. They burned the books in an incinerator.** The Historian has never yet found *any* record *anywhere* that *any* member of the AAAS objected to this method of disposing of heresy. Dr. Reich was one of the people who thought he had found evidence of the "psychic energy."

Thou shalt not discover or hallucinate psychic energy. Dig?

Dr. Hyman was even more sarcastic about teleportation than about psychic energy. Teleportation is what you call it when something arrives somewhere and you can't figure out how it got there. For instance, if the Wright Brothers had kept the airplane a secret, and I arrived in New York a few hours after you knew I was in Los Angeles that would be a teleportation, because you coudln't explain it.

Teleportation is *possible* if and only if there are scientific principles we have not yet discovered. It is *probable* if and only if you accept the evidence cited by various persons who aver that they have witnessed teleportations.

Frankly, since this is obviously Gonzo Journalism anyway, the Author was personally inclined to consider teleportation *possible,* because he doubted very much that primate brains had evolved to the point, in 1980, where they knew all the laws of the universe. Some things probably can move around by methods we do not understand. On the other hand, the Author does not consider teleportation *probable,* because the evidence cited for it by people who claim to have seen it is not quite as good as the evidence, say, that there were two Oswalds in Dallas on November 22, 1963, and considerably less good than the evidence that objects in earth's gravitational field accelerate at 32 feet per second per second unless some other forces are acting on them.

Nonetheless, Dr. Hyman sounded, and many members of the Triple-A-S sound, as if the idea of teleportation is not only improbable but impossible. The only logical justification for that position would seem to be that they are personally convinced they know *all* the laws of the universe already.

Blessed are the meek, but they will never get to sit on an AAAS panel on Science and Pseudoscience.

The best catalog of teleportations, or alleged teleportations, can be found in the books of Charles Fort—*The Book of the Damned, New Lands, Lo!* and *Wild Talents,* if you are interested. Fort collected literally thousands of cases of Damned Things appearing where they couldn't or shouldn't appear. Some of his cases come from newspapers, not the most reliable source of scientific data, but a lot of them come from scientific journals, too.

Fort himself didn't know what to make of his data. Since he was willing to be offensive to theologians as well as to scientists, he said that if "God" was moving all these things around, we should consider the possibility that "God" is a mental case.

Different maps for different chaps. Different semantic funnels for different reality-tunnels.

The next speaker was an astronomer named E. C. Krupp from Griffith Observatory. The Novelist, who had recently created an astronomer from Griffith named Bertha Van Ation, found Dr. Krupp tame by comparison.

Bertha Van Ation (who only exists in the Novelist's perverted imagination, remember) had discovered two new planets and named them Mickey and Goofy, because it makes an amusing crescendo effect when you name the planets in order from the sun: Mercury, Venus, Earth, Mars, Jupiter, Saturn, Uranus, Neptune, Pluto, Mickey and Goofy.

Mr. Krupp did not look like the sort of man who would name two new planets Mickey and Goofy. He had horn-rimmed spectacles and might have been the kind of chess master who plays sixty games simultaneously, winning fifty-nine.

Krupp quickly set to the business at hand, which was smiting Erich Von Daniken. Krupp smote Von Daniken hip and thigh, as the authors of King James might say; then he smote him some more, for good measure. When he was through smiting, everybody on the scene must have agreed that Von Daniken had been smote very thoroughly. One imagined Krupp standing over Von Daniken's body, announcing with quiet dignity, "You see? I am finished; he is quite dead now."

Krupp smote Von Daniken's arithmetic, which was all wrong, and his scholarship, which was slipshod at best, and his integrity, which is questionable even to those who try hardest to be charitable in judging our fellow humans. It was very professional smiting, but the Journalist had encountered it all before, in an occult journal called *Gnostica* which had smote Von Daniken, by cataloging the same errors in his works, several years ago. It is hard to think Krupp ever read *Gnostica*, however, since it is an "occult" journal and always has words like *"witchcraft"* and *"tantra"* and *"sex magick"* on the cover. One couldn't help wondering, though, if Krupp had read somebody who read *Gnostica*.

Of course, it is remarkably easy to smite Von Daniken, whose books are a virtual encyclopedia of how *not* to prove an argument. His arithmetic usually is off by a factor of ten or more; his scholarship is careless at best and suspiciously opportunistic always; and he has a way of railing against his critics that reminds one inescapably of another Teutonic dogmatist a few decades ago railing against International Jewry.

The only trouble with smiting Von Daniken is that his particular heresy—the idea that extraterrestrials may have visited this planet—has been espoused by many theorists whose writings are much more scholarly, careful and scientifically honest than his. This list includes Robert K. G. Temple, an English astronomer who thinks people from Sirius visited here around 4,000 years ago; Jacques Bergier, a French physicist who believes we might have been visited many times; Duncan Lunan, a Scots astronomer who has suggested that there's been a probe from Epsilon Boötis in our solar system for several centuries; and many others. One can't escape the feeling that it is easier to smite Von Daniken than any of these men, but that an attempt to smite *them* would yield more light and less heat.

Krupp was not above using a Cheap Shot, which was unnecessary, considering how vulnerable Von Daniken is to serious criticism. The Cheap Shot consisted of putting a photo of Erich Von Daniken on the screen and asking,

"Would you buy a used car from this man?" Nearly everybody in the audience, of course, laughed scornfully, to show what smart apples they were.

This offended the Journalist, who is also a Psychologist part time. It is a well-documented fact that liars do not look like liars; that is, people shown photos of a random group of individuals cannot pick out the liars. They can't even pick out the criminals, for that matter. But domesticated primates like to *think* they can read each other this way and if you show them a picture of a saint and tell them he is an ax-murderer, they will all say, and maybe believe, that they can see the "viciousness" in his eyes. If you lectured against Krupp for a half hour, and then showed a picture of Krupp, asking "Would you buy a used car from this man," most of the audience would believe they could see the dishonesty in his face.

That's a Cheap Shot.

Krupp then went on to employ the sociology of knowledge, which attempts to psychoanalyze ideas. The sociology of knowledge, objectively pursued, seeks to determine why people believe what they believe. It is seldom pursued in that objective way; it is more often used to invalidate an opponent by showing that he or she has *ulterior motives.*

Krupp proposed that people who believe earth has been visited by Outsiders believe so because this gives them psychological gratifications.

That's the tempting thing about the sociology of knowledge; you can use it anywhere. Marx originally used it to explain why everybody wasn't a Marxist, but you can use it to explain anybody who has an idea you don't like. Even Von Daniken, if he were in the audience and fast enough with a riposte, might suggest that Krupp is an Isolationist (believes we've never been visited) because that gives Krupp certain psychological gratifications. Indeed, the Sociobiologist thought of that himself. Domesticated primates are very territorial, and it fills them with anxiety and rage if Outsiders seem to be impinging on their turf. The thought of such Outsiders is likely to spook the herd. Better we should argue about one another's motivations than actually look at the evidence that such Outsiders might be peeping through the windows or oozing down the chimney, right?

It was by now clear that the panelists thus far were all Liberals. The difference between Liberals and Conservatives is that Conservatives want to hit heretics on the head with blunt instruments but Liberals want to treat them for mental illness. The chief function of the panel, the Psychologist thought, was to disseminate the Liberal view that heretics are mentally ill. "Pathological science" is the science of the mentally ill.

The next speaker, a grim fellow with dark hair, dark mustache and even dark eyebrows, looked like a physician on soap opera telling the heroine she only has three months to live. He was Rodney Stark of the University of Washington, and his subject was the geography of heresy.

Most heretics, he said, live on the Pacific Coast—no great surprise; we even have a joke out here that California is like granola because it consists of equal parts of fruits, nuts, and flakes. But Stark was replete with surveys, charts and data of all kinds, which proved that the situation was not just Californian. It goes all the way up and down the Coast, he said: Washington, Oregon and even Alaska are infected.

There are more cults here than anywhere else, Stark said, with charts and graphs to back him up. Most of the mail to *Fate* magazine—the journal of organized, or disorganized, heresy—comes from these states. There are more astrologers listed in the phone books of our major cities than in any of the cities east of the Rockies. Furthermore, membership in the orthodox churches is lower out here than elsewhere in the country.

It all sounded very much like Timothy Leary's argument, in his book, *Intelligence Agents,* that the mutant innovative genes have been moving steadily westward for the past 30,000 years and are now all piled up on top of one another on the Pacific Coast, with no place left to go but Outer Space.

But Stark didn't go that far, of course. He gave no indication of thinking all the weirdness on the Coast is part of an evolutionary movement. He was content to note merely that there was a neuro-geography of heresy and that the heresiarchs have all landed in the Wild West.

Finally, the high point of the morning arrived, in the form of The Amazing Randi, as he styles himself. Randi looks like Santa Claus and talks like the late Sen. Joseph R. McCarthy (Rep.-Wis.). Randi is not a Liberal by any definition but a real, old-fashioned, honest-to-Cthulhu Conservative, fire-breathing variety. He wants to hit the heretics on the head with a blunt instrument.

You see, The Amazing Randi is of that school of thought which holds that he and his friends have the only "real" reality-labyrinth on the planet. All proponents of alternative reality-labyrinths are therefore, *by definition,* a bunch of *sneaks, cheats* and *liars.* This is the best rhetorical stance for a heresy-hunter, since it is rooted deeply in primate psychology. It is much easier to rile up a herd of primates by hollering "That gang over there are sneaks, cheats and liars" than by the Liberal path of saying "That gang has an honest difference of opinion with us." Hitler pointed this out in *Mein Kampf,* every demagogue knows it, and Randi, an old showman, plays it to the hilt.

Randi's presentation consisted of saying five different ways that the heretics are a bunch of dishonest bastards who lie morning, noon and night, and lie in their sleep just to keep in practice. Then, in case there were any dullards in the audience who hadn't gotten his message, Randi said it again, five more ways. The Journalist hadn't heard such oratory since Jim Garrison was in his heyday, finding new Kennedy assassins every second newsbreak. It was a smashing performance, and the Sociobiologist was convinced that most of the audience were breathing harder and starting to tense their muscles before it was half over. Primate mob psychology at its most primitive.

Of course, Randi was a bit unclear about who he was attacking. He kept referring to the heretics as "parapsychologists," but most of the people and groups he denounced were not parapsychologists or any kind of psychologists. But parapsychologist has evidently become a generic term in Randi's mind; it means anyone who reports anything he doesn't want to believe. His chief targets, for instance, were Drs. Harold Puthoff and Russell Targ, who are not parapsychologists but physicists. Later on, speaking to Dr. Jack Sarfatti in the audience, Randi said, "I know you. You're a parapsychologist." Dr. Sarfatti is also a physicist, not a parapsychologist. Such details are unimportant to Randi.

"Parapsychology" means to Randi what "communist" meant to Joe McCarthy or "male chauvinist" means to Gloria Steinem. It means he doesn't like your ideas.

Randi's vendetta against Drs. Puthoff and Targ is so long, tangled and replete with accusations and counter-accusations that it sounds like the plot of one of my novels. Among other things, he hates them for saying that Uri Geller can bend metal by *wishing* it bent. Puthoff and Targ deny they said this. Whenever the matter comes up, they quote their report on Geller in *Nature* magazine, in which they wrote, "Although metal bending by Geller has been observed in our laboratory, we have not been able to combine such observations with adequately controlled experiments to obtain data sufficient to support the paranormal hypothesis." That seems to mean that they saw him bend metal, but the conditions were not such that they could rule out the possibility he was doing it by trickery.

Randi refuses to believe this, and continues to damn and blast them for saying Geller did it by *wishing* it. He has a good source for this; the source happens to be his own book, *The Magic of Uri Geller*, in which he says they said it was done by wishing.

Randi has natural pride of authorship. Between what he says they said, and what they actually said, he prefers to believe what he says they said.

The debate between Randi and Drs. Puthoff and Targ is all on that level. There are two versions of *everything*. They have different claims about when Randi sent them a certain letter, about who was where in their laboratory during certain experiments, even about whether so solid and easily identifiable a person as astronaut Captain Edgar D. Mitchell was on the scene when Puthoff and Targ tested Geller.

As Abbie Hoffman once said, there seems to be a lot of different realities going around these days.

When Randi got through roasting Puthoff and Targ again, he performed some magic for the audience; he was a professional magician before he became a professional heresy-hunter. He got a volunteer from the audience and performed "psychic surgery" like the shamans in the Philippines. Randi claimed that because this performance was a fake, all similar performances must be fakes. There seems to be an undistributed middle in that syllogism; or does the fact that one duck is brown prove all ducks are brown, and does one counterfeit dollar bill prove that all dollar bills are counterfeit?

The Psychologist had even more trouble with Randi's idea that "psychic surgery" and other shamanic tricks are necessarily bad for their customers. Everybody knows about the placebo effect—give a patient a powder and tell him it will make him better, and quite often he *will* get better. In a tribal society which has heard of surgery but doesn't have any surgeons, "psychic surgery" could very well work as a *dramatized* placebo. Since Randi didn't quote any statistics on how people respond to psychic surgery (scientific method is strangely alien to him), one only had his bald assertion that it didn't work as placebo.

In fact, we do know that all forms of faith healing, healing by suggestion, etc. work best with people who want to get well, who are, as it were, looking for an excuse to get well. For instance, *Medical Sciences Bulletin* reported (14 September 1979) that these are the types who respond best to placebos. (The types who want to stay sick ignore placebos along with all other therapies.) It seems likely that the people who resort to psychic surgery are the former type, looking for an excuse to get well, and that those who would not respond to it wouldn't even try it.

For that matter, the Psychologist (perhaps beginning to relapse into the Satirical Novelist again) could not help wondering how much surgery in our own society is a similar form of dramatized placebo. After all, with inflation rising every time you take a breath, many a doctor may find himself wondering if you need your right leg as much as he needs a new Cadillac; and there are few doctors who doubt that they need new Cadillacs every year, along with a condo in the city, a summer home in the country, various other chunks of real estate, and the other amenities of the alpha male in a domesticated primate horde.

But such thoughts are subversive, and maybe even treasonous; better to dump on the medicine men of other primate packs, especially if they live in jungles and can be considered primitive.

Randi did a few more tricks; the best of them involved Jack Sarfatti, the physicist whom he insisted on calling a parapsychologist. Randi had Dr. Sarfatti pick a word at random from a piece of paper which he, Randi, alleged was a newspaper story. The Journalist, of course, assumed or guessed that it was not a newspaper story at all but a clever fake and that Sarfatti's choice was limited to very few words indeed.

In any event, Sarfatti picked the word "wander," and Randi, after stalling for a few minutes with various subterfuges, instructed Sarfatti to look under his chair. And, lo and behold, under the chair was a letter by Randi, dated several days earlier and sealed by a Notary, saying in effect "I knew you would pick 'wander.' "

Things got a bit vague for several minutes after that, while the Author turned into an Amateur Magician and figured out how Randi did it. He finally decided that it was a variation on the old trick in which you ask the subject to pick a number from one to four. He picks, say, three, and you announced, "Look under the ash-tray." Under the ash-tray is, of course, a note saying, "I knew you would pick three."

The gimmick is that there are three other notes, under other objects in the room, saying respectively, "I knew you would pick one," "I knew you would pick two," and "I knew you would pick four." Simple, see?

For Randi's variation, you would need a confederate seated behind Dr. Sarfatti to attach the appropriate letter after the word was chosen. The Journalist did some snooping later and learned from another physicist, Saul Paul Sirag, that the man seated behind Sarfatti was a known friend or associate, and hence a possible confederate, of Randi's.

Randi hates to have his tricks revealed. He'll probably denounce Saul Paul Sirag as a parapsychologist if he reads this.

When the Amateur Magician had satisfied himself that he had the basic gimmick in this trick, and turned himself back into a Journalist, Randi was in the midst of his peroration. In case anybody in the room had missed the point of his earlier remarks about parapsychologists, he repeated all over again all of his denunciations of them, building up steam as he went along, and you could see he had the audience in the palm of his hand—if he had ended with "Let's get a rope and string the bastards up right now!" anything could have happened.

And so, as Lemuel Gulliver might have concluded a report on the seminar, these *Learned* Men, having Inquir'd deeply into the *Case* for the *Opposition,* discover'd that the Opposition had no Case and were *Devoid* of *Merit,* which was what they Suspected all along, and they arriv'd at this *Happy Conclusion* by the most Economical and Nice of all Methods of Enquiry, which was that they did not Invite the Opposition to confuse *Matters* by Participating in the Discussion.

Most of the audience marched out, smiles of contentment adorning their faces. They had heard what they came to hear, and all was well in their little worlds.

Then the heretics got up from the sinner's bench, one by one, and made their short five-minute rebuttals. Dr. Sinclair watched them closely, with one eye on his wristwatch, to make sure they didn't go over their time limit.

Dr. Russell Targ, of Stanford Research Institute, spoke even less than five minutes. He said that everything Randi had said about his research was untrue, that the reports on the research were in print in *Nature* magazine, and that anybody who wanted to form an impartial judgment should go and look up the reports. He sounded tired, as if he had said that so many times that he was getting bored with hearing himself say it again.

Randi jumped up again and called Dr. Targ about seventeen kinds of liar, including damned liar and revolving liar and plain and fancy liar.

Dr. Harold Puthoff, also of SRI, got up and made pretty much the same speech as Dr. Targ, inviting people to read their reports instead of just accepting Randi's version of their research.

Randi jumped up again and called Dr. Puthoff twenty-three kinds of rascal and scoundrel.

Dr. Geoffrey Mishlove got up and said that everything Randi had said about Ted Serios, the man who allegedly can put pictures on film by wishing them there, was inaccurate.

You can imagine what Randi said about Dr. Mishlove. Randi's vocabulary of abuse is rather limited and repetitious.

Dr. Jack Sarfatti got up and spoke for nearly the full five minutes allotted to heretics. He said that the only reason for believing in the so-called paranormal was if it happened to you so often that it got to be normal. He said that it had happened to him that often. He also said that he was working on a new theory of quantum mechanics that might explain *why* these so-called paranormal events happen. Then his time was up and he had to leave the stage.

Nobody at the AAAS wanted to hear a theory that suggested the paranormal was normal, anyway.

In fact, by then almost everybody had left the room and the heretics were making speeches to one another. One of them, a physicist named Milton Freedman, got the mike for a while and argued that *some* UFOs (he was very emphatic about some) are interstellar spaceships. By the time he finished, the room was almost as barren of population as the Mohave desert and he was virtually addressing the four walls.

And so the Novelist got a pretty good idea of how the French Academy of Sciences would have reacted to Sigismundo Celine's blasphemous meteorite in 1780. They would have appointed a panel of five men who didn't believe in meteorites, to debate the issue impartially. One of them would suggest that pro-meteorite people should also be heard, but he wouldn't insist on it. Another would produce statistics showing that meteorites are most commonly reported in a part of France known to be full of kooks. A third would denounce a book on meteorites by a man who also believed in the Tooth Fairy. And a professional demagogue would round out the day by denouncing people who see meteorites as scoundrels, rascals, liars, fools and lousy no-good bastards in general.

The Sociobiologist also profited from the day. He acquired quite a few notes for his projected non-fiction opus, *Dominance Rituals Among Domesticated Primates.*

The Journalist found the whole experience entertaining but hardly edifying.

The Psychologist made one final note: "After this article appears in print, Randi will claim I'm a parapsychologist." You can bet money on that, by the way; remember what happened to anybody who questioned Joe McCarthy's tactics.

The Philosopher asked himself how much his prejudice in favor of heretics and oddballs in general had warped his view of what happened. The answer, he believed, was: not much, actually. He didn't trust Von Daniken himself, he thought quantum physics was far stranger (and therefore more Romantic) than parapsychology, and he didn't claim to be able to guess whether any of the individual heretics were right or wrong. (It would take another twenty years of research before anybody could form an objective opinion about that anyway.) What was fascinating was the way in which the alpha males, in typical mammalian fashion, relegated the heretics to bottom-dog or outcaste position.

He wandered over to a symposium on Sociobiology held by a group called SCIENCE FOR THE PEOPLE. They all hated Sociobiology as much as Randi hates parapsychology. They hated it because Sociobiologists take Darwin seriously and really believe we are a primate species, with all the usual primate habits. They went on and on, denouncing Sociobiology as degrading to humanity and perdurably Damned. And all the time they were saying these things the Journalist kept imagining he was watching another gang of primates working themselves up into a rage against a rival tribe. It was like the cast of *Planet of the Apes* arguing about their own superiority and rationality. The Journalist had to leave because he was afraid he would start to laugh in an uncontrollable way and, what with his press card saying HIGH TIMES, they might think he was on some kind of weird drugs.

King Herod's Lust

Wilde, like a stallion, loved a boy
and counted the rosary of prison years
repenting every werewolf kiss
middle-aged need had bestowed on youth

in a city of loneliness Edgar Poe
starved his soul till his skin bleached white

William Hierens wrote in lipstick on a wall
the secret language of our century
and a little girl's body chopped in four
he left behind for tabloids and the priests

the perverse poet in the London fog
Jack wrote in blood six odes to love

the infant Hitler was deprived of love
and, through processes that a Jew named Freud
has taught us all to understand,
six million people later died

Ravechal, who threw bombs in restaurants,
said, "There are no innocent bourgeoisie."

and not until the blade of time
can shave selfishness from the poor self's need
will the need for love be a loving thing
and the naked flesh not a naked cage

NEUROGEOGRAPHY
OF CONSPIRACY

The implicit claim, on the contrary, is
that a multitude of conspiracies contend
in the night . . . Conspiracy is the normal
continuation of normal politics by normal
means.

Carl Oglesby,
The Yankee and Cowboy War

This chapter is intended to be suggestive, not conclusive, and anybody who takes its theories as dogmas is hereby denounced in advance as a damned fool.

1. Human knowledge, in terms of countable scientific facts, has been doubling for quite a long time.* As we have already seen, Georges Anderla found that such countable hard knowledge doubled between the birth of Christ and 1500 A.D., a period of 1500 years. It doubled again by 1750 A.D., a period of 250 years; again by 1900, a period of 150 years; again by 1950, a period of 50 years; and again by 1960, a period of 10 years. This sum total of known facts doubled again by 1967, a period of 7 years, and again by 1973, a period of 6 years. In all probability it has doubled again since then. (The source for these Anderla statistics is *Conquest of Death*, by Dr. Alvin Silverstein.)

2. I assume (along with Buckminster Fuller, Alfred Korzybski, Phil Laut and others) that *Real Knowledge produces Real Capital* (known resources, plants in operation, etc.)—as

---

*No statement is made or intended about *wisdom*, which is private, not public, and somewhat more mysterious.

distinct from Money Capital which is produced and manipulated by interested cliques. If Real Knowledge produces Real Capital, Real Capital should also be increasing. Indeed, ever since economists started collecting figures in the 18th century, Real Capital has shown a steady tendency to double every generation. (See, for instance, *The Iron Sun*, Adrian Berry.)

3. The distinction between Real Capital and Money Capital can be elucidated simply. If all the *Real Capital* (which includes things like maps and roads as well as factories) were to disappear overnight, we would be back in the Middle Ages. If all the *Money Capital* (cash, stocks, bonds, etc.) disappeared, there would be one hell of a fight over who "owned" what, but *the world would be the same.* All the hard, tangible, real wealth would still be there.

4. Real Capital is produced rapidly where Real Knowledge is being produced rapidly. Money Capital follows, and is basically a series of bookkeeping maneuvers by clever persons to obtain ownership-control of the Real Capital.

5. *At every period of history, there seems to be one geographical center where Real Knowledge is accumulating rapidly.* Over milleniums, this center tends to move westward (and mildly northward). For instance, the alloying of metals, which produced the Bronze Age and "civilization-as-we-know-it" appeared first around Cambodia-Thailand ca. 3500 B.C. Vast agricultural enterprises, pyramids, etc. followed rapidly in the same area. This "hot center" spread northward to China and westward to India over the next thousand years. Later, the "hot center" was Babylon, then Egypt; then Greece. Since the birth of Christ, we have seen it move from Rome upward to Venice, then to Germany, then to England, etc. (Source: *Critical Path*, Buckminster Fuller.)

6. The shift of Real Capital has also moved steadily westward, as we could expect from our hypothesis that Real Knowledge *produces* Real Capital. This was first documented at length by Brooks Adams in *The Law of Civilization and Decay*, 1892, at which time Adams saw Real Capital in

transition from London to New York. **The transition was completed during the doubling of knowledge 1900–1950, by which time the British Empire had collapsed and the American Empire had arisen.**

7. To visualize this process concretely, mentally compare the growth of Real Capital and Real Knowledge at certain key spots in space-time. Think of Egypt 1000 B.C., Rome 100 A.D., the great Italian city-states 1500 A.D., London 1750 A.D., New York-New England 1800–1900 A.D.

8. The causes of this Westward Shift are obscure. Timothy Leary suggests that, since the Earth turns from west to east, the persons with ornery and innovative genes go *against* the inertial drag, and move east to west. This may be a romantic speculation, but it is worth considering. From a Jungian orientation, assuming a "collective unconscious," it is interesting to me that every mythology I have ever studied assumes the "land of the blessed" is in the west. The African termite does not know why it migrates, leaves one hill and founds another; perhaps some genetic signalling system controls all migrations, insect, bird and mammalian, including the human.

9. Politics is "normal mammalian behavior" as Timothy Leary says: struggles over territory and resources.

10. War is "the continuation of politics by other means" (Clausewitz).

11. In the murky area between politics and war many *conspiracies* "contend in the night." Conspiracy (clandestine politics) is most common in **transition periods when the "hot center" of wealth-and-knowledge is moving from one place (more easterly) to another place (more westerly).**

12. The Westward Shift is still continuing. The principal battle within the U.S. has been for some time the struggle between Old Eastern Capital (New York-New England), called the Yankees by Carl Oglesby, and New Western Capital (Sun Belt-Texas-California), called the Cowboys by Oglesby.

The first battle between Yankees and Cowboys was the "free silver" movement of the 1890s, which is now mostly obliterated from national memory. (All that most people recall of that struggle is that William Jennings Bryan gave a speech ending with the resonant line, "You shall not crucify mankind upon a cross of gold." Few know what that metaphor meant.) What was at issue was the Cowboy demand for free coinage of silver, which was desirable because they had found a great many silver mines in the West. This free coinage would have accelerated the transfer of Western Real Capital into Money-Capital, expanded the currency, and created a source of Money Capital **independent of Yankee (Wall Street) control.** The Yankees naturally opposed that, and, being the stronger party at that time, they won the battle, despite Bryan's rhetoric. Free coinage of silver was forbidden. The Cowboys had to wait half a century to achieve enough power to challenge the Yankees seriously.

13. The Yankee-Cowboy coalition was united (against Roosevelt, labor unions, radicalism-in-general, and, finally, the Axis powers) until the end of World War II. The coalition has been fighting, and coming together for common interests, and then fighting again, ever since then.

14. Consider the last two decades.

1960: The Yankees control the White House, through Kennedy; the Cowboys grow disgruntled. By **"lucky accident"** a "deranged lone assassin" shoots Kennedy (or the Cowboys create that impression, while actually staging a *coup*). The Cowboys rule, under Lyndon Johnson, until 1968. The Yankees, controlling most of the media, encourage the anti-war movement and destroy Johnson's "image." He is soon perceived as barbaric, almost monstrous, by nearly everybody. All is in readiness for another Yankee take-over, via Bobby Kennedy. Another **lucky accident** for the Cowboys, or another plot. Bobby dies.

The Cowboys continue to rule, via Richard Nixon. The Yankee media go to work on Nixon's "image"; Watergate leaks through a thousand funnels. (Oglesby actually argues that Watergate was bungled and intended to explode, by a Yankee-C.I.A. operative, to destroy Nixon. Maybe.)

1974: Interregnum of Gerald Ford; attempts to reunite Yankees and Cowboys. (But Ford was a member of the Yankee-financed Bilderbergers.)

1976: Election of Jimmy Carter, Yankee-Trilateral tool. For the first time since JFK's death, the Yankees are in control. Everything mysteriously goes wrong for Carter . . .

1980: Election of Reagan, for the Cowboys, with George Bush, long-time Yankee, as Vice-President. The present appears as a time in which the coalition is coming back together —Yankees and Cowboys united against all the rest of the world.

15 As George Washington once said, "Nations have no permanent allies, only permanent interests." The same is true of conspiracies. Where all monistic conspiracy theories go crazy is in ignoring this elementary neuropolitical fact. Oglesby is sane in recognizing that *sometimes* Yankees fight Yankees and Cowboys fight Cowboys more than each fights the other.

16. As Thorstein Veblen noted nearly 80 years ago, there is also a split in the ruling elite between *financiers* and *engineers*. The financier (in pure form: in abstraction, for convenience of analysis) tends to think only of profit returned on each dollar invested. The engineer thinks, more commonly, in terms of doing a better job. The engineer thinks this way for the same reason composers want to write a better symphony or novelists to write a better novel; it's what they love to do; it is their joy and not just their job.

17. In the auto industry, for instance, the engineers dominated for a long time—as typified by Henry Ford—and the emphasis was always on building a car that *performed* better. Since the late 1930s, the financiers have been in charge, and emphasis is on building a car that *sells* better. (See John Keats, *Insolent Chariots;* R. Buckminster Fuller, *Critical Path.*)

18. This conflict, observed by Veblen, is still continuing. *The Future of the Intellectuals and the Rise of the New Class* by Alvin Gould says it is happening *everywhere* in

American business. "Techno-managerial types" (Gould's term for Veblen's engineers) are struggling to wrest control of corporations from financial interests. The technocrats, Gould says, perceive themselves as more scientific and also more humanitarian than the old elite, whom they see as motivated only by selfish profiteering.

19. There is a tendency for amalgamation of the interests of techno-managerial types with Cowboys, but it is emphatically not an identity yet. Differences remain, e.g., the Reaganite old Cowboys all expect an eventual nuclear showdown with Russia (and some of them seem to think "the sooner, the better"); the technofolk believe nobody can survive that, and tend to support Yankee efforts toward *detente.*

20. The entrepreneur tends to be more in tune with the engineers than with the financiers. Henry Ford and Howard Hughes, for instance, were engineers originally; in old age, their feuds with the Yankees had grown so bitter that their opinions about the Yankee establishment are more extreme than anything uttered by the New Left or even by the John Birch Society.

21. California has more scientists than any other state and more Nobel Prizewinners than all other states combined. Large-to-dominant parts of the space industry and microprocessor industry are in California. So-called "California culture" is a reality-labyrinth of "crazy heresies"—i.e., all forms of orthodoxy are breaking down, all new ideas (from the pathological to the seeds of the Next Paradigm) flourish on the entire Pacific Coast. All of this suggests Rome ca. 1 A.D., the Italian city-states ca. 1500 A.D., and England ca. 1750 A.D. In short, the "hot center" is in Cowboy territory.

22. Pessimism is rampant in cultures that are on their way out, as Nietzsche first noted. The official culture of the Yankee world and Eastern Seaboard intellectuals is entirely pessimistic—in Nietzsche's term, *decadent.* Optimism flourishes only west of the Rockies.

23. From all of the above, one can expect that the Cowboys will eventually triumph over the Yankees; the engineers

will more and more be drawn into the Cowboy nexus; the Westward Shift of Real Knowledge/Real Capital will continue and Money Capital will follow it. The next "Wall Street" will be in the Sun Belt.

24. Contrary to Marx, all of history is not the story of class warfare. That is minor theme, and only heats up at a few critical points. Most of history is a war between **competing groups of ruling elites,** all of whom escalate politics into conspiracy when feeling threatened.

25. The increase of Real Knowledge/Real Capital tends to make each successive elite more powerful than previous elites. (The multi-nationals control more today than the Robber Barons controlled in the 19th century; they, in turn, controlled more than the Venetian bankers ca. 1500, who controlled more than a feudal king, etc.)

26. This increase in Knowledge/Capital, despite conspiracies, tends always to raise the general living standard of the whole society. E.g., taking the living standard of the top one percent of U.S. society in 1900 as a working definition of affluence, Bucky Fuller has calculated that 40 percent had reached that standard by the 1920s, 50 percent by the 1960s, and 60 percent by 1980. (*Critical Path*, Fuller.)

27. More players than ever enter the Power Struggle. E.g., the number of millionaires in the U.S. *doubled* between 1971 and 1979. (Fuller, ibid.)

28. The number of real and imaginary conspiracies increases in periods when an old elite is fighting a new elite and more players are entering the game. This is because the difference between a *conspiracy* and an *affinity-group* is subtle and shifting. A true conspiracy practices clandestinism (deception) as policy; but every affinity group has a tendency to suspect every other affinity group of doing exactly that; and those who are open and honest at one time may decide they have to be devious and clandestine at another time (to protect themselves). *Conspiracy is contagious* and so is worrying about it.

29. At such times, theories about totally imaginary conspiracies also escalate, because (a) times of transition make people nervous and uncertain, (b) nervous and uncertain people tend to become at least a little bit paranoid, (c) most people most of the time follow their own prejudices and anxieties much more than any technique for ascertaining objective facts, and (d) most people have no knowledge of the techniques or self-disciplines necessary to the search for objective facts.

30. All clandestine groups (whether the commercial-economic conspiracies we have been discussing, or the Secret Police ubiquitous these days in every nation) have a vested interest in spreading false conspiracy theories, for two reasons: (a) The more disinformation in circulation, the harder it is for outsiders to find out what is really going on, and (b) it is always handy to provide a scapegoat to distract people from what *you* are doing.

31. Every conspiracy collapses eventually, because of Washington's Law ("no permanent allies, only permanent interests"), and also because of the psychological likelihood that those who are superlatively clever at deceiving others become equally clever at deceiving themselves. *Disinformation eats those who create it.* This may be why each Power Elite eventually loses out to a new Power Elite. The most successful conspiracy, at a date, is in process of becoming the stupidest conspiracy, because everybody is bribed, cajoled, threatened, or deluded into telling it only what it wants to hear.* Eventually, its view of the world is totally skewed by its own prejudices, and it thinks and acts in a bizarre "lunatic" manner, not meshing with reality. (Nixon's Syndrome.)

32. Conspiracy is *entropic* behavior, since it is blocking the flow of information. Science, as an ideal, is based on *negative entropy*, rapid exchange of information. To the extent

---

*The National Security Act was passed in 1948. Dr. Reich's books were burned six years later in 1954. The conspiracy to suppress Velikovsky followed. Leary was imprisoned in 1970. Now there is a war on laetrile, etc. "The Empire never ended."

that various conspiracies (within, above or in symbiosis with government) have persuaded scientists to cooperate in conspiratorial behavior, blocking the flow of information—TOP SECRET, YOUR EYES ONLY, etc.—science has become entropic and, in a radical sense, *un*-scientific.

33. The major battle of the 1980s will be over the control of microprocessors. The techno-managerial elite, the American Civil Liberties Union and those scientists who are true to the spirit of science will unite to attempt to *accelerate the flow of information* with these marvelous new tools. All conspiracies, and all scientists working for conspiracies, will attempt censorship, blockage, legal restrictions. Marshall Mc-Luhan long ago predicted that we were entering an age of information; it is now happening. How much freedom of electronic "speech" we are allowed in the next ten years will determine whether conspiracy or the Bill of Rights is going to dominate our future.

F A S T   F O R W A R D

Space Agriculture—food grown in space for earthside consumption—will be practical by 2010.

Source: Brian O'Leary, astronaut-physicist

IS GOD A DOPE?
OR JUST PLAIN CLUMSY?

In the writings of many contemporary psychics and mystics (e.g., Gopi Krishna, Shri Rajneesh, Frannie Steiger, John White, Hal Lindsay and several dozen others whose names I have mercifully forgotten) there is a repeated prediction that the Earth is about to be afflicted with unprecedented calamities, including every possible type of natural catastrophe from earthquakes to Pole Shifts. Most of humanity will be destroyed, these seers inform us cheerfully. This cataclysm is referred to, by many of them, as "the Great Purification" or "the Great Cleansing," and it is supposed to be a punishment for our sins.

I find the morality and theology of this Doomsday Brigade highly questionable. A large part of the Native American population was exterminated in the 19th century; I cannot regard that as a "Great Cleansing" or believe that the Indians were being punished for their sins. Nor can I think of Hitler's death camps, or Hiroshima or Nagasaki, as "Great Purifications." And I can't make myself believe that the millions killed by plagues, cancers, natural catastrophes, etc., throughout history were all singled out by some Cosmic Intelligence for punishment, while the survivors were preserved due to their virtues. To accept the idea of "God" implicit in such views is logically to hold that everybody hit by a car deserved it, and we should not try to get him to a hospital and save his life, since "God" wants him dead.

I don't know who are the worst sinners on this planet, but I am quite sure that if a Higher Intelligence wanted to exterminate them, It would find a very precise method of locating each one separately. After all, even Lee Harvey Oswald—

assuming the official version of the Kennedy assassination—only hit one innocent bystander while aiming at JFK. To assume that Divinity would employ earthquakes and Pole Shifts to "get" (say) Richard Nixon, carelessly murdering millions of innocent children and harmless old ladies and dogs and cats in the process, is absolutely and ineluctably to state that your idea of God is of a cosmic imbecile.

F A S T   F O R W A R D

Using modern technology to the utmost, we could give every human being on this planet a standard of living comparable to that of a billionaire.

Source: *Critical Path*, R. Buckminster Fuller

Zen Telegrams

921P PST JAN 2 69 LA679 MA 792
M CA634 PDF CHICAGO ILL 2
GREGORY HILL, DLY 75
1543-ROSALIA RD 260 LOSA

DISREGARD THIS TELEGRAM
AND CONTINUE WHAT YOU
WERE DOING BEFORE IT WAS
RECEIVED

ROBERT ANTON WILSON

C L KC555 PD
TDL SAN ANDREAS CANYON CALIF NFT
ROBERT ANTON WILSON DLR ONLY, DLY
1444 WEST FARGO CHGO 60626

CAN'T. FORGOT WHAT IT WAS.
PLEASE ADVISE.

(CFM SIG MAL2)

GREGORY HILL

System Compatibility Testing

Dada is not dead!
Watch your overcoat!
Andre Breton

Einstein created Relativity by asking *operational* questions: "What operations do we perform to find out what time it is?" "What operations do we perform to find out the distance between point A and point B?" etc. It was then obvious that time and space are relative to the persons making the measurements and their velocities with respect to whatever they were measuring.

The same operational methodology was introduced into the definition of intelligence by English mathematician Alan Turing. Confronted with the question, "How intelligent is a given machine?" Turing operationally asked how we go about estimating intelligence. He decided that if we are confronted with signals on a console, *or words on a printed page for that matter,* we estimate the intelligence of the sender by how much information we have received or decoded.*

Let us be a little more specific about this.

Any associated supporting element must utilize and be functionally interwoven with the evolution of specifications

---

*This is the foundation of Dr. Timothy Leary's definition, "Intelligence is information received, decoded and transmitted by a structure."

over a given time period. However, the incorporation of additional project parameters is further complexified when taking into account sophisticated implementation methodologies. Similarly, the characterization of specific criteria adds explicit performance limits to more cost-effective concepts. *A large portion of the interface coordination communication adds overriding performance constraints to system compatibility testing.*

The product configuration baseline is further complexified when taking into account any *discrete* configuration at this point in time.

In this regard, any associated supporting element adds overriding performance constraints to system compatibility testing. The independent functional principle maximizes the probability of project success and minimizes the cost and time required for more cost-effective concepts. The fully integrated test program presents extremely interesting challenges to system compatibility testing.

The incorporation of additional project parameters adds explicit performance limits to the structural design. **A large portion of the interface coordination communication maximizes the probability of project success and minimizes the cost and time required for any discrete configuration at this point in time.**

The last four paragraphs—the section between the two triangles—was entirely composed by a computer.

The computer was programmed by my friend, Geoffrey Baldwin, who calls this program "The Buzz-Word Generator." It works by having four "buckets," each of which contains ten phrases. A short input generates random numbers, which are fed to a larger program which selects the numbered phrase from one of the "buckets," after checking that it hasn't been used too recently, and then goes to the next bucket for the next random phrase; and so on. The rules of English grammar have been fed in earlier, so that the machine only strings together these phrases according to correct rules of style.

What emerges, as you can see, bears an uncanny resemblance to the sort of language that flows in torrential floods through all bureaucracies and large corporations these days.

In this regard, any associated supporting element adds *overriding performance constraints to system compatibility testing.* Or, as Blake Williams says, the final war will be between Pavlov's Dog and Schrödinger's Cat.

BUCKY FULLER:
Aborting The
Self-Destruct Mechanism

One evening in September 1927, a young man who felt like a total failure stood on the shore of Lake Michigan in Chicago, contemplating suicide. "I said to myself, 'I've done the best I know how and it hasn't worked.' I really thought I was some kind of freak," he recalled later. The lake wind was freezing cold, but he stayed there many hours, arguing with God and the Universe and himself. He was 32, penniless and unemployed; he had just failed in business and was still grieving over the death of his daughter five years earlier. He did not think it likely that he would ever be competent enough to support his wife and newborn daughter.

That man was, of course, Richard Buckminster Fuller, and everybody knows the happy ending: he is now about as widely respected and loved internationally as Leonardo, Beethoven or Santa Claus. He has had so many prestigious positions that even a partial listing makes him sound like a science-fiction polymath: science and technology consultant at *Fortune*, chief mechanical engineer of the U.S. Board of Economic Warfare, Norton Professor of Poetry at Harvard, assistant to the director at Phelps Dodge Corporation, dean at Black Mountain College . . . the list goes on for pages. Alden Hatch, one of Fuller's biographers, claims that no other living American is so well known in every nation on the planet.

The radomes (radar domes) of our Distant Early Warning system were designed by Fuller; more than 300,000 of his large geodesic domes are standing, on every continent, making him the most visible architect in history. Models of the domes are to be found in classrooms and museums, playgrounds and sundry shops. His Dymaxion map projection (which contains no distortion of land areas) is becoming almost as familiar as the Mercator projection and gives a more accurate view of our planet. In a recent issue of *The Futurist,* Barbara Marx Hubbard spoke for millions of his admirers when she wrote, "R. Buckminster Fuller is emerging as an archetype of the future: a new image of man . . . Fuller's very state of being is a historical event."

Yet for all that, Bucky Fuller (as he wants everybody to call him) is—like Einstein in the 1930s—much more admired than he is understood. Many still regard him as a brilliant crank, tossing off marvelous inventions and incoherent philosophical notions like a Ben Franklin on acid. His most important scientific tenet—which is that he has discovered the coordinate system of nature—is regarded with skepticism by most mathematicians. His social philosophy, from which all his work actually grows, is often dismissed as utopian and "visionary."

The coordinate system of nature, according to Fuller, is synergetics, the synergetic-energetic geometry he has been developing since 1927. This bold assertion, if it were accepted, could set Fuller high in the history of scientific discovery, but it is rejected by many mathematicians. One of the new revelations and great shocks of nineteenth-century geometry—that Euclid's system was not the only possible one—was demonstrated when Gauss, Lobachevski and Riemann each produced a non-Euclidean geometry. Since then, there has been general agreement that the Universe does not use one geometry; we can invent many geometries depending on our purposes and the magnitude of the space being studied. Fuller sounds naive in claiming to have the "real" geometry.

Nonetheless, Bucky will not back down. He argues that our world view has been hung up on the cube, but that Nature is more profitably looked at by means of a coordinate system based on triangles, rather than squares. Nature is always economical, he says. His geometry is designed with this economy in mind; that is why his famous domes, based on Nature's most stable shape, the triangle, deliver more stability per pound than similar structures enclosing the same space. Fuller also has a few vindicated prophecies to support him. He said that all chemical structures would turn out to be synergetic in his sense—that is, tetrahedral and more stable than might be predicted from their individual structural parts —and all organic chemicals are now recognized to be structured that way.

In the first volume of *Synergetics,* he has attempted to show that the DNA helix can be modeled by interlocked tetrahedra of the type he calls tetrahelixes and that the paradoxes of quantum theory will disappear if physicists will recast their models in synergetic geometry.

Bucky Fuller comes from an old New England family of rugged individualists and heretics. His grandfather, an ardent abolitionist, insisted on enlisting in the Union Army even though he was over 40; he was killed in battle. His great-aunt was the transcendentalist philosopher-editor Margaret Fuller, who was a close friend of Emerson and Thoreau and first published Emerson in the *Dial.* It was from this stubborn Yankee background that Fuller developed the intransigent idealism that made him feel like a "freak" in the materialistic 1920s. He still speaks with profound respect of his grandmother, who taught him to live always by the Golden Rule, no matter what other people did.

When Bucky first went into business (after two expulsions from Harvard—for unruly behavior—and then redeeming himself by serving as a naval officer in World War I), he found that nobody believed in that Golden Rule stuff. Social Darwinism—popularly known as "dog eat dog"—was the dominant philosophy in corporate life, and Bucky was confused and pained by it.

On the night in September 1927 when he contemplated suicide at the age of 32, Fuller decided to live the rest of his life as an experiment. He wouldn't believe anything anybody had told him—Golden Rule, dog eat dog or any of it—and would try to find out, by experience only, what could be physically demonstrated to work.

In the year following that decision, Bucky stopped talking entirely, like many mystics in the East. He insists that he had nothing "mystical" in mind. "I was simply trying to free myself of conditioned reflexes," he says. He had met pioneer semanticist Count Alfred Korzybski shortly before and was convinced that Korzybski was correct in his claim that language structures caused conditioned associations—mechanical reactions that keep us locked into certain perceptual grids. Fuller tried to break these grids, to find out what a person "of average intelligence" could accomplish if guided only by personal observation and experiment.

When Bucky started talking again, he had begun to develop that peculiar jargon that has continued to dazzle, enlighten and annoy various audiences. He refuses to say "up" or "down" because there is no up or down in the Universe; he insists that astronauts go "out," "in" and "around," not "up." He always writes "Universe" instead of "the Universe" because Einstein's principle of nonsimultaneity shows Universe is not a static *thing* but a process. His adjectives often begin with "omni-" because in this way he checks himself, as he goes along, to see if a statement is a general principle or only a special case. And, of course, some of his coinages—*tensegrity,* for tensional integrity, and *Spaceship Earth*—have begun to creep into general speech, thereby, if Korzybski was right, altering our perceptions.

One of Fuller's first experience-gained insights, he asserts, was that the Golden Rule was practical, after all. "I had been positively effective in producing life-advantaging wealth—which realistically protected, nurtured and accommodated X number of human lives for Y numbers of forward days—only when I was doing so entirely for others and not for myself . . . Thus it became obvious that if I worked always and only for all humanity, I would be optimally effective."

With such an attitude, Fuller quickly acquired a reputation as a brilliant crackpot. Although he held various important jobs in government and industry and published a few books, and his designs were frequently hailed in "world of the future" newspaper features, most of his inventions remained in the prototype stage for decades. Nobody would invest in his work, not because his designs were radical but because he had decided that his 1920s failures were due to his having compromised his principles, and he would not compromise again.

Then, in 1954, a study by the U.S. Marine Corps determined that Fuller's geodesic domes could be delivered by helicopter *anywhere*, usually could be fully erected within hours and were superior in strength to conventional "box" housing. By the early 1960s, the domes were appearing everywhere and the intransigent idealist was suddenly famous. His prestige has been climbing ever since, and he has become an idol to millions everywhere on the planet.

Fuller (who, like that other notable generalist Thomas Jefferson, keeps records of *everything*) calculated in 1981 that he had traveled 3.5 million miles so far, to teach, to lecture, to advise or to supervise design projects. He has been around the world, he notes, 48 times—making it cheaper for him to rent cars than to own them. Typically, he has exact figures on that: he owned 43 cars before discovering it was cheaper to rent and has rented 100 since then.

In person, Bucky Fuller is not impressive at first glance: he is shorter than average, a bit bowlegged and somewhat deaf, and, because of weak vision, he stares at you through glasses so thick that his eyes seem to bulge gigantically like those of a B-movie extraterrestrial. When he starts talking, all that changes immediately. You are either totally confused or enormously excited; most often, you are both confused and excited. "He puts you in a trance," said one engineer after a Fuller seminar. "No," said another, "he wakes you out of your trance."

The problem with Fuller's talk, as well as his books, is that he has always been a comprehensivist. "If nature wanted us to be specialists," he likes to say, "we'd be born with one eye and a jeweler's lens attached." He refuses to discuss any subject without relating it to other subjects. When asked in an interview in 1980 if he had one most important idea, he snapped, "Absolutely not. There is no 'one most important thing,' since every system in Universe is plural and at minimum six. No, I have never found one most important thing. I deal in Universe always and only."

Universe, according to Fuller is both physical and metaphysical. This statement creates communication problems at once, since most scientists are inclined to follow the logical positivists in classifying "metaphysical" as "meaningless," but Fuller does have a meaning for it. Universe is "at minimum six" relationships because every seeming "object" is actually a relationship; the minimal three-dimensional object is a tetrahedron, which has six edges. Fuller calls objects "knots" (a pattern integrity) to emphasize that they are plural and structured. Knots are made up of trajectories that cross and create stable patterns. Thus he says that "matter is knots in energy," crystallizing the basic discoveries of relativity and quantum mechanics into one poetic image.

In addition to these local "knots," Universe also contains generalized scientific principles, or laws. These are metaphysical, in Fuller's semantics, because they are eternal, weightless, massless, temperatureless and omni-interaccommodative—the characteristics traditionally assigned to the metaphyscial.

Since Claude Shannon's *A Mathematical Theory of Communication* (1948), Fuller has seen a basic link between these synergetic general principles and Shannon's definition of information. Shannon showed that information is an ordering of energy and therefore the mathematical reciprocal of entropy, which is the tendency of energy to grow disordered (chaotic). If you shuffle a deck of cards, disorder will increase, because that's the most probable outcome. If you order the deck red-black-red-black or king to ace or whatever, you are creating information, in Shannon's sense. Information is nowadays sometimes called negentropy, or negative entropy.

According to Fuller, bringing order to natural systems—creating information—is a synergetic process. Since we humans are problem solvers, we serve a local function in opposing entropy by creating information or coherence. We can do this only by understanding the metaphysical (that is, omnipresent) generalized principles of Universe.

These generalized principles, when applied to specific local problems, become technology. It therefore follows that the more generalized principles we understand, the more local problems we can solve. According to Fuller, an artifact for solving a class of problems is *wealth*.

IBM is rich, he would insist, not because it has money but because it has general principles encoded into problem-solving artifacts that can cope with so many forward days of so many human lives. The Arabs are suddenly rich, not because they have money but because they have petroleum, an artifact that temporarily solves the problem of mass transportation, and, even more important, they have acquired the know-how needed for its production and distribution. In general, Fuller sees wealth as the product of **energy times intelligence**; energy turned into artifacts that "advantage" human life.

It follows that with enough knowledge of generalized principles, the wealth of the human species can be expanded indefinitely. This is Fuller's explanation of the fact, well known to statistical economists, that real capital (plants in operation, known resources, etc.) has doubled every generation since records were first kept in the eighteenth century.

Fuller describes this process as **ephemeralization**—every scientific advance allows us to "do more with less." The automobile, for instance, is only 15 percent efficient—it wastes 85 percent of the energy it uses. The fuel cells invented by NASA are 80 percent efficient—they waste only 20 percent of their energy. Fuller documents the idea that this kind of real capital does tend to turn into money capital with graphs showing the increase of affluence in industrial and post-industrial nations. Taking the average living standard of the top 1 percent of the U.S. population in 1900 as a standard of affluence, for instance, he has a graph showing that 40 percent of the U.S. population had reached that level by 1920, 50 percent by 1950, 60 percent by 1970.

Fuller believes that we now have the "energy slaves" (technological artifacts) to make the whole human race the equivalent of billionaires. He also believes that most of these energy slaves are invisible—known only to specialists, such as mathematicians, metallurgists and physicists. Thus he grimly predicts that the rulers of the major powers, not knowing of this potential abundance, are competing more fiercely for the resources they *do* know about and are leading us to the brink of "evolutionary emergency."

In fact, Fuller picked the 1980s as the decade of emergency over 30 years ago. With his typical faith in his own prognostications and his total logic, he gave up smoking in 1945 to increase the probability that he would survive into the 1980s to work on the problems of this oncoming emergency. At 86, he now says the evolutionary crises will peak in the next eight years, by 1989. There is no doubt that he fully intends to be here then.

Bucky's notorious "optimism" is regarded by many as naiveté. Fuller insists that he is not an optimist but a realist. The work of his World Game project, he says, has demonstrated that we *can* increase real capital to the point where everybody will have the tools (energy slaves) to live like a Rockefeller. The World Game's inventory of resources shows, he insists, that *we can achieve this only by international cooperation.* "War is obsolete," he says. "Our only real problems are ignorance, fear and greed: the rulers and the ruled are both largely unaware of the actual facts of our resources and our options."

One of Fuller's key examples of the desirability of cooperation and the relative entropy involved in competition concerns his proposed worldwide electrical grid. This has been one of his major preoccupations for over 40 years, since he first decided that such a grid would be possible given the improvements in technology that his graphs led him to expect by around 1960. These improvements did arrive approximately on schedule, in 1961, when 1,500-mile delivery reach was attained. Since then Fuller has been trying to sell the world-grid idea to the governments of the United States, Canada and the U.S.S.R., because the first step toward such a grid would be the linkup of the U.S., the Canadian and the Russian electrical networks across the Bering Strait, "advantaging all without disadvantaging any."

Canadian Prime Minister Pierre Trudeau is in favor of the idea, and Russian scientists recently pronounced it "feasible" and "desirable." If it is achieved (and Fuller believes it will be, within the next eight years), the odds shift in favor of survival and against nuclear war, since it will profit no nation to blow up the other end of its own electrical system.

But until such synergistic opportunities are recognized, Fuller says, power structures will continue to plot against each other, and a war of unprecedented horror remains a real possibility. In short, he sees the whole human species standing as he stood on that memorable night in 1927, hovering between self-destruction and a serious attempt to make the Golden Rule work. Having aborted his own self-destruct tendencies that night, he feels he must demonstrate that humanity does have the option to be a success.

"I am not deceiving humanity," Fuller repeats again and again. "Everything I say can be proven." He points to the incredulity of the board of directors of General Motors when Walter Reuther, then president of the United Auto Workers, told them in 1953 that they would make money if they granted their workers the highest salary increases in American history. Reuther had this worked out on a computer and challenged the board to check it on their own computer. When they did, they found he was right and granted the increases. The explanation: rich workers buy more cars than poor workers. Fuller similarly insists that any computer anywhere will confirm what he and his World Game team assert:

international cooperation will make us all very rich very fast; international competition will very likely blow us to hell.

The next eight years will determine very clearly whether Bucky Fuller is the most scientifically precise social scientist in the history of this planet or just a starry-eyed visionary.

He has no doubt of the outcome. "The human mind was designed for total success in Universe," he tells every audience. When an interviewer challenged the claim that he was a person of "average intelligence" when he began his life experiment that night in 1927, Fuller said, "Repeat my experiment. Try living by those rules. I am no special child of God. Each of you is."

Bucky's Crystal Ball

Ever since 1928, Buckminster Fuller has been making outrageous predictions—that come true. He does not depend on intuition alone but carefully charts trends that reveal the future.

One of Fuller's earliest graphs compares the weight of aircraft engines with their horsepower from the time of the Wright Brothers up to 1928. Since weight steadily decreased in comparison with the horsepower increase, he projected that more and more horsepower would continue to come out of lighter and lighter engines; hence aircraft would carry more and more people over greater and greater distances. As early as 1928, he predicted a "one-town world," which became reality by the 1960s with extensive air-traffic networks.

Fuller also charted modes of travel since the Stone Age: foot, horseback, sailing ship, steamship and airplane. He forecast that by 1985 we would have the technology to cross oceans in *seconds*. If you consider space travel, this is close to being true.

Making a graph in the late 1920s of the time lag between discoveries and their practical applications, Fuller found that in electronics a new paradigm is technologically applied within two years and in aerodynamics, within five. In the auto industry, the lag increases to 10 years; in railroading, 15 years; in office-building design, 25 years; in single-family dwellings, 50 years. This led him to expect that his then-new architectural innovations—mass-manufacturable homes—would be widely applied to large buildings in the 1950s, as happened, and to homes in the 1980s, which he anticipates.

Armed with his charts, Fuller was inspired to prepare for upcoming breakthroughs. He designed housing for moon colonists before anybody walked on the moon. He proposed doors to be operated by electric eyes a year before such technology was invented. When electrical power could be transmitted only 350 miles, he foresaw a 1,500-mile reach for the 1960s and designed his worldwide grid, which he now expects will be implemented by 1989.

AMERICAN LIFE BOMB
WENT AUTHORITARIAN

Shannon's basic equation for information—in grossly simplified terms is:

$$-H = p_1 \log_e p_1 + p_2 \log_e p_2 \ldots \ldots + p_n \log_e p_n$$

To translate into English, p_1 is the probability that you can predict or guess the first signal; p_2 is the probability that you can predict the second signal; and so on, to p_n, the last signal. The logarithms ($\log_e$) are part of the equation because this is a transcendental function; it does not accumulate additively but synergetically. (A logarithm is an exponent of a base number.)*

H is the information in the transmission.

H is negative, written $-H$, because the information is the reciprocal (the reverse) of your probability of guessing what is coming next. What you *can* guess is not information.

"Anybody, kindly take my shoes off."

Information accumulates non-additively (logarithmically) because it is a reverse of probability which is a non-linear function. Every time you cut up a piece of prose, you add to the richness of the information:

"Contactees agree that it is always a flickering by violence, because its nature is a violent one."

"It's a bitch under human bombs."

Hitler's favorite metaphor was *strong medicine*, an image that appears over and over in *Mein Kampf* and again and again in his speeches. It turned out to be poison, but you

---

*Each new "bit" of information does not add linearly onto past knowledge but raises it to a new order of coherence. Hence the "Jumping Jesus" phenomenon: 1 j, 2 j, 4 j, 8 j, etc.

can't say he didn't warn us. *Learn to read metaphor and you can read history,* as Vico knew.

"Some of the people, or humanoids, in the sexual attitudes of the parents . . ."

"Oh, sir, get the doll a former Black Panther."

Shannon also experimented with picking words out of a hat at random, to see how much coherence would appear by chance. Modern quantum theorists might say he was contacting the Hidden Variables of David Bohm, the implicate order, the primordial in-form-ation. The first coherent near-sentence he obtained was: FRONTAL ATTACK ON AN ENGLISH WRITER.

In a similar experiment in 1955, I obtained AMERICAN LIFE BOMB WENT AUTHORITARIAN. Some of you may remember that sentence sneaking its way into *Illuminatus!* later, with no hint that it was a mechanical process, not a human, "thinking."

"Rats and alligators did not explicitly control symbols," Sir John Babcock ventured.

"We did not fall because of moral error. We fell in the pre-Einsteinian murk," Blake Williams told him calmly.

Of course, there are dangers. All experiments can get out of control and run amok. Too much information (which amounts to an absence of redundancy, in Shannon's phrase) can create the equivalent of noise. The mind abandons the search for meaning, drowning in an ocean of *too much meaning.* The editor of cut-ups must be aware of this and keep a certain amount of redundancy in the stew:

"You betcha you ass. 'God' has a penis? Such developments indicate that in sex, as elsewhere, The West Point Class of 1915 was on board Flight 553."

Verbal structures *contain information and radiate energy.* We read only because the radiated energy activates resonant energy in the brain. Some of these bits ideologically and financially split into no *"real" space* anywhere.

When William Butler Yeats contacted a group of discarnate spirits (or his own unconscious) in 1929, he expected important philosophical messages. The spirits quickly corrected him. "**We have come,**" they said, "**to bring you metaphors for poetry.**"

As Korzybski noted, those who control symbols control humanity. The Junkyard Dog activates thoughts, feelings and (apparent) sense impressions. Think of junk, garbage, the discard of civilization. The outskirts of any large city, anygoddamnwhere. Newspapers blowing in the streets. Rats peering with hungry eyes from an old Model-T Ford. Now add your basic mean sonofabitch dog. You are "in" the Reagan tunnel-reality.

"No, there's a handcuff on them."

"Freud called it Thanatos, Offisa Pup."

(the mystical bliss-out)

"But one clings . . . within the temples . . ."

"We have come," they said. "Euclidean space. Or territory. First. We pass through Chinatown."

". . . gives milk and glows in the dark . . . the power of love . . ." Crowley grinned enigmatically.

The mother, at this stage of libidinal development, grills and inspects the steaks. The unbearability of light or color suggested we cook them his way and among the working masses. I was speechless. Everybody understands Mickey Mouse cities—the gate in time—

Gold Rush days: I thought surely this ship shifts in the direction of the mother.

Elijah brought a boy his Presidency. The exaggerated severeness like a 12-inch penis . . . raised his beef at Gettysburg . . . the eye of Horus designed to avoid feedback . . .

In conclusion, the brain-change experiences before they start the Bingo Game. I Am Under Attack . . . a bunch of *sneaks, cheats* and *liars* . . . Different realities if you need your right leg.

Creatures lacking eyes . . . a crazy man bleeding in the snow . . . The Westward Shift is fucking. I felt the Garden of Eden in the afternoon . . .

A great symphony expanding toward infinity from Colorado.

"You encounter them over and over because they are repeating brain loops," Simon Moon told Babcock.

General Haig said, "I'm in charge here." 553 left Washington and headed for Chicago. It doesn't care whether you like the trip or not.

Lt. Calley's lawyers are the crown of thorns in the London fog.

"A boy in mini-skirts?" Joyce protested.

"The near sight of Dorothy Hunt . . ." Einstein nodded.

"Poetry bits concern a handcuff on them!" Crowley jeered.

"I am loothing them and the Supreme Court would operate here," Sheriff Carpenter said, still frightened.

People will stop *outside your body.* I refer to the unknown phenomenon "out there." McCord said this threat included the definite skeletons in sexual attitudes.

Dorothy Hunt, according to McCord, had been given $100,000 in bribe money before Flight 553. On her body, after the crash, only $10,000 was found. The other $90,000 was never accounted for.

Carl Oglesby makes a good case that the Watergate scandals were deliberately "leaked" by a Yankee coalition to drive Nixon out of the White House, Nixon being a representative of Western "Cowboy" money.

General Haig attributed it to an intellectual error: that of taking the phenomenal world as real.

Sherman Skolnick, a free-lance anti-crime crusader in Chicago, had previously unearthed mob connections of several Illinois judges, forcing their resignations. He investigated Flight 553 and argued that the evidence indicated sabotage.

"On or about November 30"—according to later testimony by James McCord—Mrs. Hunt had told McCord that if more bribe money were not forthcoming quickly, her husband would "blow the White House out of the water." McCord said this threat included the definite statement that

"Hunt had information which would impeach the President."

The permutations and combinations of these bits contain $10^{2,783,000}$ possible variations. That's $10^{2,783,000}$ possible models of "you" and the "external" world.

"Some of these bits included the definite statement Nixon keeps worrying," Celine clarified.

"The other $90,000 at Gettysburg and liars soon . . . in a whirlwind . . ." Mozart sounded unconvinced.

"A whorehouse is not a metaphor," Blake said.

"A battle with Death and a conquest leading to Marilyn Chambers . . . to prepare them for zero gravity . . ."

"Information had asked Gysin a question," said Joe Malik.

"O bitter ending! Pass on in silence induced by certain yoga exercizes," Crowley told Joyce.

Take a chair. Any goddamn chair. Right where you are sitting now. Get up and look at it. You don't see the chair alone. Millions of light signals are being integrated very bloody fast and they all pass through the verbal centers. An English-speaker DOES NOT see the same chair as a Hopi-speaker or a Chinese-speaker, as Benjamin Whorf demonstrated. You see what language and metaphor allow you to see.

Mozart could see the whole symphony before he started writing because it was a form of information; that is, the structure was present in the first *bit* that came to him.

Shannon's equation, then, is saying that you can only produce information by breaking the lines of habitual association. Like Burroughs, Shannon found the whole key by stringing words together in a *random* process. What then appears, as in this experiment, is the implicate order—the continuous acts of creation out of which the space-time manifold appears.

And this is the subject of the Jupiter Symphony, got it?

"I am impressed by the facts that the Jonestown zombies used the same poison—cyanide—as the Nazis in our novel, and that they held their own Götterdämmerung during the first American stage production of *Illuminatus!*/cut/

"Captain **Whitehouse**, the pilot of Flight 553, was found to have 3.9 micrograms per milliliter of **cyanide** in his blood, an extremely high amount"/cut/

"Hunt said he would blow the **White House** out of the water"

If you can read metaphor, you can read history.

Coming unstuck in time—or in space—so-called out-of-body experience—is possible only when certain repeating tape loops are cut, disconnected, and reconnected in new ways.

I think of this book as a machine, in the sense that Le Corbusier described a house as a "dwelling machine." These lines of words and images are a mechanism, a crafted tool, to disconnect the user from all maps and models whatsoever. The machine doesn't care who you are or what you think. Plug it in and it does its job. The job here is to put you in the head space where an ouija board predicts the future; where you are living in a foreign country and it all begins to seem normal to you, so that a visitor from your home country suddenly looks alien and strange; where a new scientific theory begins to make sense; where a work of art that had seemed a hoax or a barbarism abruptly becomes beautiful and full of meaning; where you are first waking up and can't remember who you are or where you are . . .

The machine does its job. It doesn't care whether you like the trip or not.

WE PASS
THROUGH CHINATOWN

Long shot of baseball field.

ANNOUNCER'S VOICE *(offscreen):* Two runs in, the Cardinals lead . . .

click, blurry lines

WILLIAM F. BUCKLEY and G. GORDON LIDDY are in the "Firing Line" chairs exchanging Deep Thoughts.

LIDDY: The professors and other bleeding-hearts think there's nothing out there but Charley the Tuna. Well, what's really out there is *Jaws!*

BUCKLEY chortles appreciatively.

click, blurry lines

Brisk, professionally detached NEWSCASTER, female, black. The usual dead-level stare into the camera.

NEWSCASTER: . . . a *chicken!* The Congressman has issued an official denial and attributed the reports to the Midwestern Dope Dealers Association. Elsewhere in the Capital, President Cthulhu again declared his faith in God.

Flash-cut: PRESIDENT CTHULHU in Press Conference Room.

CTHULHU: He sent manna in the desert. He parted the Red Sea. He . . .

click, blurry lines

Three MEN wearing earphones. Location indefinite.

FIRST MAN: I don't think it will happen. You have to look at the whole picture to get some perspective. Of course, we can't be certain at this early stage but . . .

click, blurry lines

Why Is The Moral Majority Like Susan Browmiller?

To me, it doesn't matter if your scapegoats are the Jews, the homosexuals, the male sex, the Masons, the Jesuits, the Welfare Parasites, the Power Elite, the female sex, the vegetarians or the Communist Party. To the extent that you *need* scapegoats, you simply have not got your brain programmed to work as an efficient problem-solving machine.

Show me a movement that doesn't hate somebody and I will join it at once.

F A S T   F O R W A R D

Thirty years ago a computer with the same functions as a human brain would have had to be the size of New York City and would have used more power than the NY subway system; today that computer would be the size of a TV set. By the end of the 1980s it will be small as the brain itself.

Source: *Micro Millenium*, Chris Evans

A Calculus of Dread

1. Worm-god, slime-god, compost earth,
   dine upon a lovely woman.
   Marilyn Monroe is earth and grass,
   not one atom of her lost, yet
   all of her is lost. This is
   a metaphor on modern poetry.

2. Worm-god, scum-god, slime god,
   compost earth, dine upon a President,
   John Fitzgerald Kennedy
   who was both brave and strong.
   This is not a metaphor. Poetry
   is more than drivel, simile and fiddle.
   Poetry does *not* accept the mystery
   that turns such men and women into grass.
   Poetry is a curse upon the mystery.

3. Put it this way: poetry
   is a spell against demons, the fear
   you feel on a cellar stair at night
   the man down the street with the eye tic
   and the foul-mouthed wife
   and you wonder about their bedroom scenes.
   Poetry answers. Those who know
   but cannot speak must *act* their poem
   in suicide, in murder, or in both.
   These lines are for
   Lee Harvey Oswald.

4. The rifleman in the tower,
   Charley Whitman,
   aimed, like a poet,
   straight at God. All
   poetry is prayer and blasphemy,
   a calculus of dread,
   affirming and rejecting
   the worm-god, scum-god,
   slime-god, dung-god,
   compost earth.

THE SEMANTICS OF "GOD"

I sometimes think that even God
Must find it something rather odd
To hear the priest invoke His name
Before they start the Bingo game

The language we use influences the thoughts we think much more than the thoughts we think influence the language we use. *We are encased in fossil metaphors; verbal chains guide us through our daily reality-labyrinth.*

Physicists, for example, spent nearly three centuries looking for a substance, *heat,* to correspond to the substantive noun, "heat"; it took a revolution in chemistry and thermodynamics before we realized that heat should not be thought of as a *noun* (a thing) but a *verb* (a process)—a relationship between the motions of molecules.

Around the turn of this century—this is all old news, even though most literary "intellectuals" still haven't heard about it—several mathematicians and philosophers who were well versed in the physical sciences began to realize consciously that *there is not necessarily a "thing" (a static and block-like entity) corresponding to every noun in our vocabulary.*

As Bertrand Russell wrote:

> The belief or unconscious conviction that all propositions are of the subject-predicate form—in other words, that every fact consists of some *thing* having some *quality*—has rendered most philosophers incapable of giving any account of the world of science and daily life. *(Italics added.)*

127

Relativity was made possible by Einstein's insight that "space" and "time" were not necessarily *things,* but were functions, relations, models.

The same de-thing-ification of the world dawned on Ernest Fenollosa, about the same time, struggling to translate Chinese poetry. Fenollosa began to get on the right track when he realized that Chinese was not a "barbarous" and "primitive" attempt to invent Indo-European grammar, but an alternative reality-labyrinth which did not divide the universe up into block-outlined things the way Aryan languages do.

And Ezra Pound based his revolutionary poetic style on Fenollosa; and all modern poetry—at least in England and America—is somewhat influenced by Pound; and, due to the idiotic Iron Curtain between the Humanities Department and the Science Department, most of these poets do not realize that their mode of perception is strictly Einsteinian.

Consider the child's riddle, "Where does your fist go when you open your hand?" This can be answered by *thinking like Einstein,* although on a less cosmic scale. That is, the child must realize that the "fist" is not a *thing* but a relationship (a "coherent synergy," Bucky Fuller would say). It is not a mere etymological felicity to say that thinking of *relations* is the first step toward thinking *Relativistically.*

Zen Buddhism arose in China, not in India, because Chinese, much more than Indo-European, is an "Einsteinian" language. Thus, the Fifth Patriarch of Zen, Hui Neng, said twelve centuries before Bucky Fuller, "From the beginning there has never been a thing." This is easy to see, if you are thinking in Chinese, but very difficult if you are thinking in Indo-European. Einstein only got to that mode of apprehension by thinking in mathematics (and in pictures, as he once confessed).

But all of this is by way of preparing the reader for a simple semantic suggestion, or rather two such suggestions:

1. Traditional ideas of theism, atheism and agnosticism would all have to be changed and redefined if we all said (and thought) "it" instead of "he" when referring to God.

Of course, Christian Scientists always pray to "Father-Mother God" (but drop back to "He" for a pronoun, because of linguistic convention) and witches and feminists say "She," but I am suggesting something more radical.

The average churchgoer in this part of the world considers *God* an oriental despot, only bigger and invisible—a sort of translucent *homo sapiens* of cosmic heft and mass. Sophisticated theologians will all agree that this is an absurdity, bordering almost on blasphemy. But this ridiculous picture results solely from the habitual use, from childhood on, of the pronoun "He" in reference to Divinity.

No modern Christian, Jew or Moslem seriously believes in the corporeality of "God." Jehovah walking around the Garden of Eden in the afternoon was recognized as an allegory, a parable, even by St. Augustine fifteen centuries ago. We are told on all sides that "God" is a spirit. A spirit does not have a beard like the elderly gent in Grandma's illustrated Bible. Nor does a spirit have any of the other gross morphological traits of masculinity.

We are also told that "God" is Love, a proposition that makes perfect sense to me as poetic shorthand for a very complex mode of perception but, again, Love does not have a beard and *is not,* but can only be *symbolized by,* Michelangelo's Giant Male Creator. (It is also not, but can be symbolized by, the White Goddess of Robert Graves.)

The Believer had better face himself and ask squarely: Do I literally believe "God" has a penis? If the answer is no, then it seems only logical to drop the ridiculous practice of referring to "God" as "He."

It is this "He," after all, which has given Judaism, Christianity and Islam that anthropomorphic cast which makes them so unattractive to the scientific mind. Dr. Gerald Wald wrote once in *Scientific American,* "I try to avoid making sentences with the word 'God' in them." What he is objecting to is clearly the dualistic anthropomorphic image of Big Daddy separate from the universe, for later he adds that when somebody else says "God" he mentally translates this as "the order of nature."

Which brings to mind a recent interview I had with Bucky Fuller.

> WILSON: Why do you always write "Universe" instead of "the Universe"?
>
> FULLER: "The" comes from *theos*, God, and "God God" seems rather redundant.
>
> WILSON: Then "God" and "Universe" mean the same to you?
>
> FULLER: "God" seems like a rather small concept to contain the exquisitely interaccommodative coherencies of Universe.

So, then: suppose the Believer begins referring to "God" as *it*. He will soon find that his statements about *it* will grow more abstract and impersonal. If he implies purpose to *it*, he will be more cautious about attributing such human (or subhuman) purposes as jealousy, authoritarianism, intolerance, vengeance or a paranoid obsession with the sexual behavior of the people down the street. Dr. Wald will find it easier to translate the Believer's statements, since "the order of nature" is more an *it* than a *He.*

The nonbeliever, in turn, may begin to wonder what, exactly, he is opposing. Certainly, nobody, not even the most rabid Bible-smashing professional atheist, can deny that all the forces, principles and laws observable in nature may be aspects of one bedrock underlying in-form-ation system or implicate order active in all times and all places. "And this," as Aquinas says, "it is customary to call God." *It* may be conscious, even; or, if not conscious as we are conscious, It may still be "intelligent" in *some* sense. Yositani Roshi, trying to explain the Zen concept of "Buddha-mind" (the closest thing Zen has to a "God"), used to say it is not far away and metaphysical but always **right where you are sitting now.** "When the room gets cold at night and you pull up the covers without waking, that is Buddha-mind acting," he said.

This "trans-personal" (or un-personalized) *It* is invoked by Lao-Tse as follows:

> Something cloudy and unclear
> Before existence and non-existence,
> Before heaven and earth,
> I do not know its name
> So I call it *Tao*

Perplexed beyond endurance by the paradoxes of quantum physics, Sir Arthur Eddington once wrote, "Something unknown is doing something we cannot understand." Alan Watts delightedly pointed out that in those words Eddington was closer to Buddhism than in all his more highfalutin' "metaphysical" verbalizations.

2. St. Anselm argued that "God" has to be bigger (more comprehensive) than any of our thoughts in order to be "God." This seems like circular reasoning or special pleading at first glance; but think about it.

In science, any new theory* has to be more comprehensive than an old theory in order to gain assent. Einstein's physics replaced Newton's only because it included more; in spatial metaphor, it was "bigger"; in a jargon I prefer, it was of a higher order of coherence. It expanded our collective omnidimensional mind.

The ultimate theory, supposing such a thing possible, would have to include all and everything.

$$T = A + B$$

where T is this hypothetical ultimate theory, A is what we presently understand, and B is what we don't understand yet.

The ultimate theory would be a theophany.

If Dr. Wald's "order of nature" is not just another superstition like Jehovah walking in the Garden—if chaos is not the only reality, on which we impose one fashionable map or model after another—if the explosive omnidimensional expansion of knowledge (1900: 8 j; 1950: 16 j; 1973: 128 j) is

---

*In this context it is worth remembering that *theory* etymologically means an analog or model of *theos*, "God."

revealing and not just *creating* a true universal coherence—
then IT, that coherence or law or synergy, always, *at a date,*
consists of both A and B, what we understand and what we
don't understand yet.

Since A + B in this case must be bigger than A (B cannot
be negative here), the "order of nature" or IT must, at any
date, be "bigger" than any theory. Only at infinity, or at the
end of time—whatever that means—can the ultimate theory
or theophany (A + B) be achieved.

Thus, IT can metaphorically be considered as an Intelligence and even as possessed by "personality" (or the cosmic
analog of "personality"), in the manner of the traditional
theist; or IT can be considered as a giant machine, as the
traditional materialist prefers; IT can be seen as a mesh of
energy or four-dimensional grid of energy or a "dance" of
energy, which are metaphors from early 20th century physics;
or IT may be visualized as an Information System, which is
the current model I happen to like; but in any of these cases,
we are in the realm of metaphor, and we are talking only
about A, what we understand (or think we understand) now,
and we haven't included, and can't include B which is by
definition what we don't understand yet.

As a relief from all such argument, I often find myself
considering IT as a great symphony or a great poem. Those
are metaphors, too, but there is no danger (I hope) that anybody will mistake them for anything else *but* metaphors.

World Without Nouns:
Part One

Post-Einsteinian theology can only begin from Bucky Fuller's proposition, "God is not a noun; God is a verb."

ECOLOGY, MALTHUS
AND MACHIAVELLI

I thought Dr. Barry Commoner was the most intelligent speaker I had heard at the American Association for the Advancement of Science convention, but when election day rolled around I couldn't bring myself to vote for him.

This was not unusual. I hadn't voted since 1964, when I voted for Lyndon Johnson (because Barry Goldwater frightened me). Johnson promptly did just about everything I had feared Goldwater might do. I remembered Nietzsche's aphorism, "The role of the intellectual in politics must always be a comic one," and refused to believe any of the bastards anymore.

In 1968, Hubert Humphrey seemed as bad as Nixon to me, since old HHH had written the bill introducing Concentration Camps to America. In 1972, George McGovern looked a lot better than Nixon, of course, but I refused to vote for another "peace-loving Democratic liberal" against another "war-mongering Republican" after 1964: I had a mildly paranoid suspicion that McGovern would do an LBJ: escalate the war, just to demonstrate again that political Image has no connection at all with political Reality. In 1976, I rooted for Carter, but refused to vote for him: I just allowed myself to hope Jimmy would win, whatever the consequences, because I wanted to see The Man Who Pardoned Nixon go down to ignominious defeat.

By election day 1980, I was ready to vote again, just to make an active, rather than passive, gesture of protest. Carter and Reagan I did not consider for a minute, because one of them was sure to win, and I didn't want to suffer again what I had experienced after "my" candidate won in 1964. I

135

intended to vote for one of the minority candidates, so that my rejection of Carter and Reagan would be visible; staying home and not voting had begun to seem esoteric to me.

I considered Zippy the Pinhead, because his slogan appealed to me—"I have the same platform as Ronald Reagan," he said, "but I'm funnier." I was also attracted to Nobody, represented by Col. Hugh Romney (USAF-ret.) a.k.a. Wavy Gravy a.k.a. Nobody's Fool. I liked the campaign stickers that said "Nobody will cut your taxes," "Nobody can represent you better than you can represent yourself," "Nobody makes better apple pie than Mom," "Nobody is perfect," and so on.

Ideologically, of course, I should have voted for Ed Clark, the Libertarian Party candidate; but I am not that kind of Libertarian, really; I don't hate poor people.

I finally voted for John Anderson, just because his speeches (with which I did not always agree) were so wonderfully weird. "The Doonesbury Candidate" did not seem to me to be trying to win, but just having a hell of a good time saying what he really thought in front of huge audiences. I *identified* with him. I have always wanted to get my ideas on television, too; and I figured that that was what was motivating him.

Yet and still, I wish Dr. Commoner had won. I don't know why I feel that way. Probably, it's because I have always harbored a deep conviction that 99 percent of what appalls me in Washington is due to the abysmal ignorance of science that prevails there. Dr. Commoner might or might not do what I would wish, but he is obviously less *ignorant* than any candidate in recent memory.

The real reason I couldn't vote for him, I think, is that any Ecologist, however sensible, is, willy-nilly, part of the Ecology Movement, part of what I call Pop Ecology, and that scares me as much as Goldwater did in 1964.

My daughter, Karuna, once said she learned the word "ecology" from the conversations of her mother and myself when she was about four, i.e., in 1959. I have actually been fascinated with ecology (and life sciences generally) since my high school days, 1946–1950; and yet Pop Ecology seems so stupid to me that I doubt that even a scientist as well-informed as Dr. Commoner can lead it out of the fanatic darkness into the rational light.

Ecological science, like all science, is relativistic, evolutionary and progressive; that is, it regards all generalizations as hypothetical and is always ready to revise them. It seeks truth but never claims to have attained all truth. Pop ecology, or ecological *mysticism*, is the reverse in all respects. It is absolutist, dogmatic and fanatical. It does not usually refer its arguments back to ecological science (except vaguely and often inaccurately); it refers back to emotions, moral judgments and the casual baggage of ill-assorted ideas that make up pop culture generally. Ecological mysticism, in short, is only rhetorically connected with the science of ecology, or any science; it is basically a crusade, a quasi-religion, an *ideology*.* It is my suspicion that the usefulness of the ideology of eco-mysticism to the ruling elite is no accident.

The tax-exempt foundations which largely finance Pop Ecology are funded by the so-called Yankee Establishment—the Eastern banking-industrial interests of whom the Rockefellers are the symbols. If this Yankee financing is not "coincidental" and "accidental" (based on purely disinterested charity)—if the ecological-mystical movement is serving Yankee banker interests—a great deal of current debate is based on deliberately created mutual misunderstanding.

Consider the following widely-published and widely-believed propositions: "There isn't enough to go around." "The Revolution of Rising Expectations, since the 18th Century, was based on fallacy." "Reason and Science are to be distrusted; they are the great enemies." "We are running out of energy." "Science destroys all it touches." "Man is

---

*See in this connection *Ecological Fantasies*, by Cy Adler, a trained marine biologist who actually understands how ecosystems operate.

vile and corrupts Nature," "We must settle for Lowered Expectations."

Whether mouthed by the Club of Rome or Friends of the Earth, this ideology has one major social effect: people who are living in misery and deprivation, who might otherwise organize to seek better lives, are persuaded to accept continued deprivation, for themselves and their children. That such stoic resignation to poverty, squalor, disease, misery, starvation, etc. is useful to ruling elites has frequently been noted by Marxists *a propos* pre-ecological mysticism; and, indeed, people can only repeat the current neo-puritan line by assuming that the benefit to the Yankee oligarchy is *totally* accidental and not the chief purpose of the promulgation of this ideology.

In criticizing the dogmas of eco-puritanism, I begin with the illuminating case of the solar-power satellites. Early in the 1970s, Prof. Gerald O'Neill of Princeton and various others began proposing that we could harvest enormous amounts of nonpolluting energy from sunlight in outer space. If the eco-puritans were chiefly concerned with substituting nonpolluting energy for polluting energy, one would expect them to consider this proposal seriously. Few did.

Most Pop Ecologists rejected solar power satellites violently and shrilly, with arguments that ranged from the superstitious (one quoted an American Indian legend that if a "house" were put in the sky, the world would end) to the moralistic-misanthropic ("I don't think humanity deserves to survive," one wrote to *Co-Evolution Quarterly*) to the barely plausible (technical problems in the original designs were alleged, but those who hit on this objection did not suggest better designs; they insisted the whole idea be abandoned). Physicist J. Peter Vajk commented on this nearly universal rejection of solar satellites by eco-puritans: "They seem to want to concentrate on all possible problems and reject all possible solutions."

Coming back down to earth—and ignoring the vast potentials of space entirely*—note that R. Buckminster Fuller and his associates at the World Game Center recently determined that we are currently using only one four-millionth of one percent (0.00000025 %) of all available energy on the surface of this planet. That is, 99.99999975 percent of available terrestrial energy is not being employed yet. This is not ideology or philosophy, but simple inventory, and Dr. Fuller insists that it can be demonstrated to anyone who will look at the data in the World Game computers. (See *Critical Path*, by R. Buckminster Fuller, and *Ho-Ping: Food for Everyone*, by Medard Gabel).

The only rationale for continuing the neo-puritan Lowered Expectations, in the light of these data, would be (a) to prove that Fuller, Gabel and their associates have been fudging or corrupting their figures—a demonstration none of the eco-puritans have attempted; or (b) a blunt assertion that most of humanity *deserves* to live in misery.

For perspective, it should be remembered that the ideology of Lowered Expectations arrived on the historical scene immediately after the upsurge of Rising Expectations. That is, after the Utopian hopes of the American Declaration of Independence and the French Declaration of the Rights of Man, almost as if in reaction, an employee of the British East India Company, Thomas Malthus, created the first "scientific" argument that the ideals of those documents could never be achieved. Malthus had discovered that at his time world population was growing faster than known resources, and he *assumed* that this would always be true, and that misery would always be the fate of the majority of humanity.

The first thing wrong with Malthus's science is that "known resources" are not given by nature; they depend on the analytical capacities of the human mind. We can never

---

*It is worth mentioning, however, that engineer G. Harry Stine has calculated that there are 10^{100} industrial processes that can be performed more cheaply and/or efficiently in space, because of the low-or-zero-gravity conditions and high-quality vacuum there.

know how many resources can be obtained from a cubic foot of the universe: all we know is how much we have found *thusfar*, at a given date. You can starve in the middle of a wheat field if your mind hasn't identified wheat as edible.

Real Wealth results from Real Knowledge, which is increasing faster all the time. (256 j, 512 j . . .)

Thus the second thing wrong with Malthus's scenario is that it is no longer true. Concretely, more energy has been found in every cubic foot of the universe than Malthus ever imagined; and, as technology has spread, each nation has spontaneously experienced a lowered birth rate after industrializing. (See again *Critical Path*, Fuller, and *Ho-Ping: Food for Everyone,* Gabel.)

Unfortunately, between the 18th century inventory of Malthus and the 20th century inventory of Fuller et al., the Malthusian philosophy had become the pragmatic working principle of the British ruling class, and a bulwark against French and American radicalism. Malthusianism-plus-Machiavellianism was then quickly learned by all ruling classes elsewhere which wished to compete with the British for world domination. This was frankly acknowledged by the "classical" political economists of that period, following Ricardo, which led to economics being dubbed "the dismal science." Benjamin Jowett, an old-fashioned humanist, voiced a normal man's reaction to this dismal science: "I have always felt a certain horror of political economists since I heard one of them say that he feared the famine of 1848 [in Ireland] would not kill more than a million people, and that would scarcely be enough to do much good." In fact, the English rulers allowed the famine to continue until it killed more than two million.

In the 1920s, Karl Haushofer studied Malthusian-Machiavellian political economy in England with Prof. H. J. Mackinder—whose coldblooded global thinking coincidentally inspired Bucky Fuller to begin thinking globally but more humanistically. Haushofer took the most amoral aspects of Mackinder's geopolitics, mingled them with Vril Society occultism, and forged the philosophy of *Realpolitik,* which Hitler adopted as part of the official Nazi ideology. The horror of the Nazi regime was so extreme that few ruling classes dare to express the Malthusian-Machiavellian philosophy openly any longer, although it is almost certainly the system within which they still do their thinking.

As expressed openly by British political economists in the 19th century, and maniacally by the Nazis, *Realpolitik* says roughly, "Since there isn't enough to go around, most people must starve. In this desperate situation, who deserves to survive and live in affluence? Only the genetically superior. We will now demonstrate that *we* are the genetically superior, because we are smart enough and bold enough to grab what we want at once."

Since the fall of Hitler, this combination of Malthus and Machiavelli is no longer acceptable to most people. A more plausible, less overtly vicious Malthusianism is needed to justify a system in which a few live in splendor and the majority are condemned to squalor. This is where neo-puritan Pop Ecology comes in.

The Pop Ecologists now state the Malthusian scenario *for* the ruling elite, since it sounds self-serving when stated *by* the elite. There is an endless chorus of "There isn't enough to go around . . . Our hopes and ideals were all naive and impossible . . . Science has failed . . . We must all make sacrifices," etc., until Lowered Expectations are drummed into everybody's head.

Of course, when it comes time to implement this philosophy through action, it always turns out that **the poor are the ones who have to make sacrifices, not the elite.** But this is more or less hidden, unless you are watching the hands that move the pea from cup to cup, and if you do notice it, you are encouraged to blame it on "those damned environmentalists." Thus, the elite gets what it wants, and anybody who doesn't like it is maneuvered by the media into attributing this to the science of ecology, the cause of environmentalism, or Ralph Nader.

The ultimate implications of eco-mysticism are explicitly stated in Theodore Roszak's *Where the Wasteland Ends.* Roszak argues that science is psychologically harmful to anybody who pursues it and culturally destructive to any nation which allows it. In short, he would take us back, not just to a medieval living standard, but to a medieval religious tyranny where those possessing what he calls *gnosis*—the Illuminati—would be entirely free of nagging criticisms based on logic or experiment. The Inquisition would not try Galileo in Roszak's ideal eco-society; a man like Galileo simply would not be allowed to exist. The similarity to the notions of Haushofer and the Vril Society is unnerving. (On the Vril Society, see L. Pauwels and J. Bergier, *The Morning of the Magicians.* On the parallels between the Vril Society and Roszakian pop ecology, see the excellent novel, *Speed of Light,* by Gwyneth Cravens.)

Or consider this quotation from Pop Ecologist Gary Snyder, "But what I'm talking about is not what critics immediately call 'the Stone Age.' As Dave Brower, the founder of Friends of the Earth, is fond of retorting, 'Heck, no, I'd just like to go back to the '20s.' Which isn't an evasion because there was almost half the existing population then, and at that time we still had a functioning system of public transportation." (*City Miner,* Spring 1979) In short, Snyder wants to "get rid of" two billion people. Those who believe that none of the Pop Ecologists realize that their proposals involve *massive starvation for the majority* should consider this quotation profoundly. Benjamin Jowett, who experienced horror at the deliberate starvation of one million-plus Irishmen, would have no words to convey his revulsion at this proposed genocide of millions.

In this context, note that the only ideology opposing eco-puritanism usually well-represented by the mass media is that of the Cowboys—new Western wealth, which is still naive and barbaric in comparison to the Yankee establishment. The Cowboy response to Pop Ecology, as to any idea they don't like, is simply to bark and growl at it; their candidate, now in the White House, is famous for allowing vast destruction of California's magnificent redwoods on the grounds that "if you've seen one redwood, you've seen them all." Other and more intelligent critiques of Pop Ecology, such as have come from some Marxists and some right-wing libertarians, are simply ignored by the media, with the consequence that ecological debate—as far as the general public knows it—is, de facto, debate between the Yankees and the Cowboys. Once again, it may be a "happy coincidence" that keeping the debate on that level is just what the elite wants, or it may be more than a "happy coincidence."

George Bernard Shaw once noted that an Englishman never believes anybody is moral unless they are uncomfortable. To the extent that Pop Ecology shares this attitude and wishes to save our souls by making us suffer, it is just another of the many forms of puritanism. To the extent, however, that it insists that abundance for all is impossible (in an age when, for the first time in history, such abundance is finally possible) it merely mirrors ruling class anxieties. **The ruling elite shares the "Robin Hood" myth with most socialists; they do not think it is possible to feed the starving without first robbing the rich.** Perhaps these ruling-class terrors and the supporting cult of Pop Ecology will both wither away when it becomes generally understood that **abundance** for all literally means abundance **for all**; that, in Fuller's words, modern technology makes it possible to advantage everybody without disadvantaging anybody.

In this context, look for a minute at some very interesting words from Glenn T. Seaborg, a representative Yankee bureaucrat, former chairman of the Atomic Energy Commission.

> American society will successfully weather its crises and emerge in the 1990s as a straight and **highly disciplined,** but happier society. Today's violence, permissiveness and self-indulgence will disappear as a result of a series of painful shocks, the first of which is the current energy crisis . . . Americans will adjust to these shortages with quiet pride and a **spartan-like** spirit. [boldface added]

Is it necessary to remark that phrases like "**highly disciplined**" and "**spartan-like**" have a rather sinister ring when coming from ruling class circles? Does anybody think it is the elite who will be called upon to make "spartan" sacrifices? Is it not possible that the eco-mysticism within this call for neofascism is a handy rationalization for the kind of authoritarianism that all elites everywhere always try to impose? And is there any real-world justification for such medievalism on a planet where, as Fuller has demonstrated, 99.99999975 percent of the energy is not yet being used?

We live in an age of *artificial* scarcity, maintained by ignorance and fear. The government has been paying farmers *not to grow food* for fifty years—while millions starve. Labor unions, business and government conspire to hold back the Microprocessor Revolution—because none of them know how to deal with the massive unemployment it will cause. (Fuller's books could tell them.) The utilities advertise continually that "solar power is at least forty years in the future" when my friend Karl Hess, and hundreds of others, already live in largely solar-powered houses. These propaganda advertisements are just a delaying action, because the utilities still haven't figured out how to put a meter between us and the sun.

And Pop Ecology, perhaps only by coincidence, keeps this madness going by insisting that scarcity is real, and nobody wonders why the Establishment pays the bill for making superstars of these merchants of gloom.

SO SOFT THIS FROM
RANDOM WORD GENERATOR

The BUNKER living room. ARCHIE, EDITH, GLORIA and MIKE are in the midst of one of their lovable arguments.

ARCHIE: And that's why they aren't white, meat-head!

Loud, hilarious laughter

ARCHIE (*delivering his clincher*): That's why you never see a white gorilla or a white chimpanzee!

MIKE: Oh, yeah? I think I'm looking at one right now!

Louder laughter

> *click, blurry lines*

ALISTAIR COOKE, seated in his usual plush chair, looking portentious.

COOKE: Well, things are not looking very promising for the Tin Woodsman, are they? But Dorothy, of course, still remains optimistic, despite the machinations of the Wicked Witch of the West. L. Frank Baum always does not know that he is participating in an art work, nor dashed a thousand kim. Mayor Diane Feinstein, in a press conference capable of capturing skybuddies due to woman formed mobile which isn't all that hard to understand. p means probability or man made static . . .

> *click, blurry lines*

ROY ROGERS in black-and-white, peering over the top of a huge rock. He fires pistol rapidly.
Cut to the man ROY shot. He holds his arm in pain and falls forward, not bleeding.

> *click, blurry lines*

Sirius Rising

The world shall sing of Mary Jane
The newscasts all go daft
The goat-god's dance will dance them down
By the power of our Craft

The spell is cast. The sign appears
Of pyramid-and-eye
Old Adam's fall becomes our spring
And death itself shall die

A new star rises in the south
Prometheus is born
Fire leaps from earth to sky
On resurrection morn

All flesh shall see it in a flash
In the twinkling of an eye
A cone of power in the stars
And death itself shall die

SILVIO GESELL

The only Utopian economist I ever liked was Silvio Gesell. Of course, Gesell was a businessman, not an academic or an ideologue, so he had some common sense. In his ideal society, there would be a *one percent tax on money,* to accelerate circulation and to discourage hoarding. At the beginning of each month, you would have to put a 1¢ postage-stamp-like sticker on each dollar you owned, but not on productively invested funds. There would thus be a strong incentive to either spend or invest everything you earned in any month before the next month began, and Gesell thought this would stimulate continuous economic growth without inflation. There would be *no other taxes,* which would allegedly keep government at a reasonable size; and this single tax would never be painful, since you would have $100 of unspent, uninvested money on hand for every $1 you owed the government. Finally, to prevent land speculation and rent-gouging, the government would be the *only* landlord, but the rents collected would be redistributed to the needy, and would be the only form of Welfare. Aside from these "socialist" or quasi-socialist measures, Gesell's system would encourage absolute unrestricted free enterprise.

I don't know if that Utopia would work as neatly in practice as it sounds in theory, but my admiration for Gesell lies elsewhere. He also stipulated that the government should allow and support internal colonies or Utopian communities where people with rival economic ideas could band together and try to make their own ideal system work.

He even said that if one of the colonies was particularly successful, its ideas should be copied in place of his own system.

The only way I can account for this wild idea is that Gesell did not regard himself as infallible. No wonder so few people have ever heard of Silvio Gesell. He didn't have the fanaticism that seems necessary to get a Utopian movement rolling on a mass scale.

F A S T   F O R W A R D

Over 600 companies in Germany and Scandinavia now have contracts in which workers must approve management decisions before they can be implemented.

Source: *Labor in the Boardroom,* James Furlong

World Without Nouns: Part Two:

Post Einsteinian psychology can only begin from Bucky Fuller's empirical self-observation, "I seem to be a verb."

WE CREATED IT
BY TALKING ABOUT IT

To be is to be related.
Charles M. Child,
Individuality in Organisms

Buckminster Fuller's synergetic geometry demonstrates that every unity is inherently plural, and at minimum six. That is, infinity is ineffable and the less we say about it the fewer idiocies we will utter; but as soon as we pull something out of infinity, something we can analyze and talk about, we find it has at least six elements or aspects.

The definite, or de-finite, is a sixford synergy.

"This information was in some way racketeer-related," McCord told the Erwin committee.

The definiteness of expressions resides in the Death Junkyard. We live in an age of *artificial* or at least transpersonal reality-tunnels. I don't say this . . . *It controls symbols.*

General Haig tells us that we have sinned. "The Empire never ended." Jesus knew all about the product configuration baseline: any associated supporting element must be balanced on her ass.

Arresting officer Sgt. Joe Friday got me all hot and bothered, now that I recall your basic mean sonofabitch dog. A few may get through to the heretic's bench.

"Roy Rogers and his horse, Trigger spent two hours at loveplay, the most intense loveplay, covering the complete gamut including the heretics in the sinners bench . . ."

The way to determine truth until the mind is enflamed by love . . .

Advances in modern science in denying the reality of perceptions—Or consider this quotation: "The awakening from robotism is no accident. Two other performers could very well work as a *dramatized* placebo."

Every tribe and nation *if enough people believe in them* —they're just not in their right minds.

"The invention of paper money will sweat, bleed, cry . . ."

"This Administration is no accident. The way to determine truth expanding toward infinity . . ."

If you follow a story inside, the Mick Jagger of 2005 again declared his faith in God.

"Two other performers like some kind of invisible ray . . . There was a picture of Jesus by Rutgers Medical School . . . Arresting officer Sgt. Joe Friday never heed of your name! Lff! So soft this awakening from robotism. Here is a partial list: The patriarchal age. This administration. In the 1920s, Karl Haushofer. Gulls. The invention of paper money in denying the reality of perceptions. Oh, sir, get those who control symbols!"

I'll bear it on me. The French in Russia. Marilyn Chambers to prepare my cold mad father. The Insect Trust. And other skeptics were cold.

Scientists: through the toy fair!

"Steaks!" Beethoven exclaimed.

"Exaggerated severeness . . ." Sigismundo Celine murmured.

"Marilyn Chambers. The next step . . ." Mozart said dreamily.

"Metal-bending by Geller has been charged with information . . . A blue lion is *possible* . . ." Einstein admitted.

". . . impressions that you keep encountering over and over, year after year," Joyce agreed emphatically.

Nor does a spirit have the whole mothering program:
Ezra Pound says, "Great literature is language charged with meaning to the utmost possible degree."

You can update that. "Meaning" is not a very precise mathematical concept. We might better say that great literature is language charged with *information*, in Shannon's sense; that is, it is *structured* unpredictability. The *Grundgestalt*, to borrow a musical term from Schoenberg, is a creative act, and cannot be known in advance of the transmission itself.

"Let me read it to you and see if it isn't designer jeans!" cried the man seated behind Sarfatti.

"Concretely, that seems to mean that *the world would be the same* . . . This hot center spread telling people to get higher . . . thinking like Einstein before Heaven and Earth . . ." added Jefferson thoughtfully.

Under the present brutal and primitive conditions *you can read history*—In the auto industry the ideas of teleportation and "psychic force"—The authors of King James might say, "Two new planets named Mickey and Goofy move from Rome upward to Venice, then to Germany—"

"A man with a lopsided pineal gland—his thought is felt 10,000 miles . . ." Danton reassured him.

"St. Augustine 25 centuries ago is *Jaws!*" Celine spat.

"I don't think it will happen . . . Experiments can get out of control and run amok . . . The vibrator, with a malfunction in the coolant system . . ." Marat added.

Krupp then went on to employ the sociology of a real Heavy: the Father of the Bubonic Plague; but, you know, its nature is a violent one . . .

"Oh, sir, get the black men, blue men, black-faced men with green bodies . . ." Mounty Babbit was giggling hysterically.

"Hairy metaphors for a potential Nazi you," said Simon.

And I rush . . . and this is my substitute . . .

"The infant Hitler was waiting for the devil to throw a knife," Crowley explained to Joyce.

WE ARE BEING INVADED BY BEINGS FROM INDEFINITE MACHINE.

"Coming . . . the China Syndrome . . ." said Calley.

Some of them never came home.

"God as a mass murderer . . . can be used to assure a definite hell . . ." Eichmann was rambling, high on hashish.

"Can't do another thing . . ." Hagbard said hopelessly.

"The whole world is the China Syndrome," Mavis agreed.

"We pass through grass," Beethoven told them.

"Say nothing to them," Clem Cotex advised.

"The Junkyard Dog went, authoritarian chicken."

Don't let Satan bring you metaphors.

TRYING FOR PIX OF THE COCK

POLICE in riot helmets. Hand-held camera moves jerkily. A man's body, bleeding badly, comes into view, on sidewalk.

NEWSCASTER'S VOICE *(female, offscreen):* . . . the Klan has denied any involvement . . .

COP waves club at CAMERA for unknown reason.

NEWSCASTER: . . . but the NAACP says . . .

click, blurry lines

Map of Ireland, Camera pans in on Dublin area.

NARRATOR'S VOICE *(offscreen):* On April 23, 1014, Brian Boru moved his armies onto the field of Clontarf, which is Gaelic for bull . . .

click, blurry lines

AL PACINO in a very dark, shadowy room.

PACINO: Shit, shit, shit!

CAMERA pans back, ACTRESS comes into view.

ACTRESS: Damn you, you motherfucker!

click, blurry lines

ED McMAHON laughing hysterically. CAMERA pans to JOHNNY CARSON, also out of control with hilarity.

CARSON: Well, I'll be a son of a (loud bleep).

click, blurry lines

GORILLA peering suspiciously from foliage toward CAMERA.

NARRATOR'S VOICE *(offscreen):* . . . a peaceful, vegetarian animal, without the violent streak found in mankind . . .

click, blurry lines

The Walking Wounded

Under the present brutal and primitive conditions on this planet, every person you meet should be regarded as one of the walking wounded. We have never seen a man or woman not slightly deranged by either anxiety or grief. We have never seen a totally sane human being.

F A S T   F O R W A R D

Fewer Americans than ever before will accept the labels of either Democrat or Republican. More than ever before list themselves as Independent.

Source: *Parties in Crises,* Scott and Hrebenar

The Watergate Syndrome

Taking somebody's money without permission is stealing, unless you work for the IRS; then it's *taxation*. Killing people en masse is homicidal mania, unless you work for the Army; then it's *National Defense*. Spying on your neighbors is invasion of privacy, unless you work for the FBI; then it's *National Security*. Running a whorehouse makes you a pimp and poisoning people makes you a murderer, unless you work for the CIA; then it's *counter-intelligence*.

Lately it is fashionable to claim that Nixon was a bit nuts toward the end of his career. I doubt it; he had merely been in government so long (1946–1974) that he had forgotten there was another America (outside Washington) where people still believed in something called common decency.

F A S T   F O R W A R D

It would take dozens of human beings with synthesizers to play an electronic symphony, but one computer can control all the synthesizers and create the symphony without human supervision.

Source: *Introduction to Computer Music*, Wayne Bateman

NEUROSEMANTIC
QUIZ ANSWERS

(Questions are on page 33.)

1. Conditionally true. *Always* true at sea level (on this planet) but not true, e.g., in the Himalayas and only true off this planet in those places that happen to correspond to sea level on this planet.

2. True, in ordinary mathematics. Not true in the quantum math employed by John von Neumann to describe subatomic events. A human-scale analog of quantum logic would be as follows: Imagine a small Southern town made up almost entirely of hard-shell Baptists. Let P = marriage and Q = pregnancy. In such a grid, PQ (marriage X pregnancy) does not equal QP (pregnancy X marriage).

3. True, of finite sets. Georg Cantor has created a "proof" that this is false when applied to transfinite sets; but not all mathematicians accept Cantor's proof. Therefore the proposition is true for finite sets and *(at this date)* indeterminate for transfinite sets.

4. However passionately you might agree with it, this proposition is neither *true* nor *false* nor *indeterminate*, since no known scientific or logical test can be applied to it. It is best regarded as *self-referential*, a statement about how the speaker's nervous system is operating. For semantic exactitude, then, it should really say, *"To me*, Raquel Welch is the most beautiful woman in the world."

5. Indeterminate. No such planet has yet been observed, but astronomers are looking for it, since gravitational math implies that it is probably there. (Note: by the time this book reaches print, the proposition might have graduated from indeterminate to true. Some statements—maybe most—are only true, false or indeterminate *at a date.*)

6. This statement appears to be neither true, nor false, nor indeterminate, since nobody can observe a colorless green idea to discover its sleeping habits. This proposition must, therefore, be considered *meaningless*.

7. Neither true nor false nor indeterminate. No instrument such as a smutometer can exist *even in principle*, so we can't measure the "dirtiness" of a film or any other artwork. This proposition, then, is as *meaningless* as the one about the colorless green ideas; and those who believe it is true seem to be confusing what is going on in their own nervous systems with what is measurably out there on the movie screen.

8. Neither true nor false nor indeterminate nor meaningless. This appears to be a *game-rule;* all players wishing to participate in the Roman Catholic game must give assent to it, or the game itself ceases to include them.

9. Neither true nor false nor indeterminate nor meaningless. This appears to be a statement about *somebody's evaluation* of Van Gogh and Picasso, confusingly formulated to look like a statement about Van Gogh and Picasso themselves.

10. Almost certainly true; but (a) it is partly true-by-definition. This law has proven itself so valuable to science that any "exception" will be most profitably handled by redefining what we mean by "closed system" instead of giving up the law itself. And (b) we should also keep in mind the very cogent arguments of Karl R. Popper *(The Logic of Scientific Discovery)* and Gregory Bateson *(Mind and Nature)*. Popper and Bateson both assert that science can never prove any law absolutely, since that would require an infinite number of experiments occupying an infinite number of years.

11. Neither true nor false nor indeterminate nor meaningless. The speaker is using multi-ordinal words to create precise imagistic-ideational information about subtle processes in his own nervous system. The result is known as *poetry* and has semantic value, in helping to see how human nervous systems operate, how many varieties of perception and self-perception are possible, and how to make neurologically meaningful reality-labyrinths that are not *limited to true or false.*

12. This appears to be failed poetry, or else the speaker has his semantic levels confused in the same manner as proposition 7.

13. This proposition cannot be evaluated as true, false, indeterminate or meaningless in itself, since it is part of a system which includes the next proposition. We can only evaluate the two together, since they refer to each other.

14. This system is now revealed as a *Strange Loop.* If it is true, it is false, and if it is false, it is true. This is not trivial. There are hundreds of such Strange Loops recognized in logic and mathematics, and it

requires sophisticated knowledge to detect them when they are not as obvious as this pair. Paul Watzlavik has argued (in *Pragmatics of Human Communication* and *How Real Is Real?*) that many types of mental illness take the form of internalizing such a Strange Loop and trying to live out its consequences. Alan Watts has proposed, even more grimly, in his *Psychotherapy East & West,* that whole societies can become trapped in such Strange Loops.

15. Neither true nor false nor indeterminate nor meaningless. This is a game-rule of Jeffersonian democracy.

16. This appears to be some kind of poetry. The speaker is urgently attempting to communicate perceptions and experiences that cannot be conveyed in ordinary language. (He had a bullet in the gut at the time.)

17. Indeterminate. Some mathematicians believe it; some do not. A rigorous proof is still being sought.

18. This is the only absolutely true statement in this whole book.

Note that each statement (whether we classify it as true, false, meaningless, indeterminate, metaphoric, game-rule or Strange Loop) will create an existential reality-labyrinth for those who believe it.

A change in language can transform our appreciation of the cosmos.
Benjamin Lee Whorf

Verbal chains guide us through our daily reality-labrinth.
R.A.W.

Mass seems to be over. Could hear them all at it. Pray for us. And pray for us. And pray for us. Good idea the repetition. Same thing with ads. Buy from us. And buy from us.
Leopold Bloom, in James Joyce's Ulysses

F A S T   F O R W A R D

If we find a way to tap into the "zero point energy" predicted in Heisenberg's equations, we can obtain from one cubic centimeter of vacuum enough energy to run every factory on earth for the next 1,000,000,000,000 years.

Source: Jack Sarfatti, Physics/Consciousness Research Group

If God hadn't wanted us to eat pussy, He wouldn't have made it look so much like a Taco.

The Earl of Nines

BY WAY OF SUMMARY

Your brain has 20 billion bits of information. The repeating loops between various bits make up your private reality-labyrinth, the thoughts, feelings and (apparent) sense impressions that you keep encountering over and over, year after year. You encounter them over and over precisely because they are repeating tape loops.

Ethnomethodology demonstrates that the loops can be broken at any point, a process technically known as *breaching*. The result is a rapid reorganization as the 20 billion bits quantum-jump to a different order of coherence. **A new "you" and a new "external world" appear in the process.**

There are $10^{2,783,000}$ possible permutations: alternative models of "you" and the "external world."

There is a potential Nazi you living in a Nazi eigenstate mean as a Junkyard Dog. There is a vegetarian you, a nudist you, a Buddhist you, a Roman Catholic you, and each has its own appropriate thoughts, feelings and (apparent) sense impressions.

Egyptian priestesses with whips lead two captured astronauts past a gaunt hieroglyphic wall.

"Pull me out. I am half crazy . . . stuck in the early 19th Century . . ." Sir James Babcock wept.

This is the cage of werewolf "space." Mickey Mouse cities grow up, including sundogs, heat inversions, swamp gas, the man behind Sarfatti.

"Image creating thoughts . . . impressions . . ."

"Shuffle them. Think of the sacred snatch," Joyce said.

From R. A. W.'s first, last and only belladonna trip, spring 1962: "We must all drink more milk before the

Nuremberg pickle that exploded in the Kennedy Administration of outer space."

"I'll slip away by Rutgers Medical School. I'll bear it on me. To remind me in all directions," said Sir John.

"To come unstuck in time, worrying that the Bay of Pigs thing will leak . . ." President Cthulhu moaned.

A private detective named Alex Bottos even claimed to have spoken to underworld sources (which he named) who had been involved in sabotaging Flight 553. Bottos was placed in a mental hospital and did not win his release until the investigation of Flight 553 had ended with an "accidental crash" verdict.

Using the cut-up method in Paris, 1957, Brion Gysin obtained AM I THAT AM I

You hardly have to add the question marks to see that the cut-up process, a semi-intelligent machine, had asked Gysin a question (AM I THAT? AM I?)

Put them all together they spell AMERICAN LIFE BOMB WENT AUTHORITARIAN IN FRONTAL ATTACK ON AN ENGLISH WRITER. AM I THAT? AM I?

"This is the Sin of Astral Projection."

"Some of these bits ideologically and financially split into a handcuff on them."

"For peace . . ." Beethoven said simply.

"Information had asked Gysin to assure a definite hell." Blake Williams explained.

I started talking to Bob to see how his trip was coming.

Over 24 different solar-power satellites. New Pentagon lies. If I have faith to move Beethoven's "Appassionata" sonata, which started in Thailand. Poetry is a second Trap, worse than Hiroshima Werewolf. Because of the Viking invasion.

The UFO-human experience is "normal mammalian rock and roll music." Something they put in those fluorides.

He said in a funny dry voice, "Death usually supervenes in American jails. Mad Dog Collective waxing sorely pissed. A battle with Death and a conquest leading to 99 44/100th percent pure Marilyn Chambers to prepare them for zero gravity."

Sir John Babcock pushed open the door and I performed Crowley's rituals onto the field of Clontarf.

Then I couldn't "find" the Old Testament God.

"It is not easy to reconcile with the dead bullock."

"I am passing out. A new star rises."

"Any set which is part of another set of which the Rockefellers are symbols . . ."

"A Discordian Pope . . . twice crucified . . ."

Definitions can be used to ensure a definite hell of a nasty shock.

"That's where. It says EAT GAS."

"The woodsy back country to you, my cold father."

Hunt had information that Shea and I were writing about the Illuminati . . . frontal attack on chicken . . . Forgot what it was . . . Brian Boru was killed by a fleeing Viking . . .

"No, there weren't any little green men for Lee Harvey Oswald."

"But I am dying."

"The big gorilla was *strong* in hashish clarity."

Von Neumann and Finkelstein escape all this extravagant modelling by merely throwing out Aristotelian logic: "In addition to a yes and no, the universe contains a maybe."

The power of love like a 12-inch penis.

There is also the position of John Archibald Wheeler, known as the participatory or observer-created universe. This sounds exactly like solipsism, but Wheeler says it isn't.

And there is the Copenhagen Interpretation, of Niels Bohr, which says in effect that the whole problem is emic— created by the symbols (mathematics) which physicists use to communicate with each other.

"The junkyard dog went authoritarian, chicken."

Ezra Pound said, "Great, damn it. The flying saucer *is* the naked skin."

But if the physicists cannot agree on what is etic and what is emic anymore than the social scientists, there remains at least the hard precision of pure mathematics?

Alas, no. There are now four geometries, with four different kinds of space—Euclidean flat space, Lobachevskian negatively curved space, Riemannian (Gaussian) positively curved space and Fullerian synergistic space. Which is the real space?

"You can mix black men, blue men, black-faced men . . . pompous and obtuse . . ."

"Hairy metaphors? That is too close!"

You got no trigger but BEINGS FROM INDEFINITE FUTURE—There are only ten of us and Negativism Himself—The problem is waiting for the devil and its wilder and funnier—Anti-environmentalist plot—Police, police, *dog biscuit!*

"Please keep him home."

"We leap . . . this is my substitute . . ."

"Concretely, ten million fighting."

"A half step back in the auto industry."

"Reserve decision in the universe . . ."

Police, police, I am dying.

"Reserve Einstein?"

"Dubious . . . wasting his time . . ."

"And this is my substitute, an unseen collaborator in a whirlwind. Throwing knives that whizzed right by."

Where these trajectories cross will predict a second signal. I don't know if that system would work. (The mystical bliss-out.) He meant to tell us that our universe arose in China, not in India.

Crying out for peace.

Skeletons in Naval uniforms. The ship appears Futuristic. The skeletons stand about aimlessly. "Exploring Mexico, the sea and sexuality . . . a unique experience in living alternatives—educational, emotional and sexual!"

"I believe God is on our side," the President said, "and He can certainly hate somebody and I will join it an once."

SL, LR, MIS ASK GREEN DREAMS TK X1826PCS
ALBUQUERQUE IS TRYING FOR PIX OF THE COCK

WE ARE IMPRISONED
BY IMAGE OF BIG DADDY

Brisk, professionally detached NEWSCASTER, male, moderately long hair, expensive blue jacket. He has that dead-level stare right into the camera that they all affect.

NEWSCASTER: . . . a *chicken!* In Washington, President Cthulhu denounced those who claim there can be no winner in a nuclear war. "I believe God is on our side," the President said, "and He can certainly reach down and stop the Russian missiles in flight just as he parted the Red Sea for M—

click, blurry lines

Black-and-white photography, ROY ROGERS and his horse, TRIGGER, at full gallop, racing desperately to some unknown destination to prevent some unknown calamity.

MUSIC: Wagern's *Valkyrie.*

click, blurry lines

Back to color photography. CLINT EASTWOOD on a horse at full gallop, racing desperately to some unknown destination to prevent some unknown calamity.

MUSIC: Wagner's *Valkyrie.*

click, blurry lines

Very cheerful ACTRESS, exhibits orgasmic ecstasy; stacked laundry in front of her.

ACTRESS: No more muddy mess! It's no problem for new CHEER . . .

click, blurry lines

MATT GOUIG 82

HAVE FUN WITH
YOUR NEW HEAD

*The ancient tradition that the world will
be consumed in fire at the end of six
thousand years is true . . . the whole creation will be consumed and appear infinite and holy, whereas it now appears
finite and corrupt.
This will come to pass by an improvement
of sensual enjoyment*

> William Blake
> The Marriage of Heaven and Hell

The patriarchal age is over. The monogamous age is over. Everything is over. *Buck Rogers* is the name of the game from here on out. As Alvin Toffler noted in *Future Shock,* there are more scientists alive and engaged in research right now than there were in all previous human history. This means that, along with everything else, human sexuality will be transformed more in the next 30 years than it has been in the previous 30,000.

Scan the acceleration of contemporary events: only ten years after Lenny Bruce was busted and hauled off to jail for saying the word "cocksucker" in public, Linda Lovelace, Georgina Spelvin, and 99 44/100 percent pure Marilyn Chambers are having their cocksucking styles shown in public and soberly evaluated by erotocritics, who sometimes score the ladies' talents on Peter-Meters.

The speed of travel has increased a hundredfold; known energy resources, a thousandfold; weaponry, a millionfold; data processing, a millionfold; and the speed of communications, ten millionfold in this century and all are still increasing. J. R. Platt of the University of Michigan, the man who made these calculations, has this comment on their import: "None of our social organizations is prepared to deal with change on such a scale. . . . We may oscillate, or we may destroy ourselves, or we may reach a high-level steady state." In other words, *2001* and *Flash Gordon* are more attuned to emerging fact than the most soberly intelligent social scientist in the college of your choice.

"We are *living* in science fiction," as poet Allen Ginsberg said years ago.

Run this through your computer: "Our future will be one wherein sex is linked to procreation even less than it is now. . . . And procreation itself will be virtually emancipated from sexual intercourse in a world of sperm banks, surrogate mothers, test-tube babies, and the utter asexuality of cloning. . . . Homosexual acts, for instance, will be seen as merely one sexual possibility among several open to every person, so long as he or she is not inhibited by contrary programming."

Now, anyone who thinks that's Dr. Tim Leary, Norman O. Brown, Charles A. Reich, or some other prophet of futurism is missing the beat of the mutation. The speaker is a *Roman Catholic theologian*—Professor Michael Valente of the department of religious studies at Seton Hall University.

Some people, of course, insist that the pendulum must swing back to the uptight ethic of yesteryear. Arnold Gingrich, editor-in-chief of *Esquire,* for instance, has prophesied such a retreat since the mid-Fifties. Even today, *Esquire* is eager to publish any neophobic Nostradamus who predicts a swing back to Gingrich's mother's notions of decorum, while in the real world, society has advanced rapidly from the nude breasts of the Fifties to the dawning of a muff-buff's paradise, as the sacred snatch itself came out from behind the staples in the late Sixties; from a hullabaloo over use of the word virgin in a Fifties film *(The Moon is Blue)* to ho-hum on-camera fucking in the Seventies; from the time that mere mention of the abortion issue was political suicide to the day when legislators legalized abortion; from the acknowledgment that homosexuality really exists to gay pride and bisexual chic; from parental agony that their kids might engage in heavy petting (1951) to worry that they might actually have intercourse (1961) to nervous curiosity over whether they're swinging both ways (1981).

"CITY HOSPITAL REPORTS RARE
CASE OF HUMAN PREGNANCY"
Newspaper headline of the 1990s

One reason the pendulum will not reverse is that it is extremely unlikely that any American woman will get pregnant accidentally after, perhaps, 1988. The contraceptive devices known to Grandma and Grandpa—mostly douches and condoms—averaged about 70 to 80 percent effectiveness; the IUDs and coils of Mom and Pop raised the protection effectiveness to 95 to 98 percent; the pill is at least 99 percent effective. Today we have voluntary sterilization—which, though 100 percent effective, is still usually irreversible—as well as a morning-after pill that it totally effective, although its side effects are questionable.

Foolproof contraception and, more socially important, the eradication of the fear of accidental pregnancy are just the overtures to the oncoming biological revolution—an upheaval that Dr. W. H. Thorpe of Cambridge University has predicted will create social consequences "at least as great as those arising from atomic energy and the H-bomb. . . . They rank in importance as high as, if not higher than, the discovery of fire, of agriculture, the development of printing, and the discovery of the wheel."

"I'm taking a half hour off this afternoon,"
says the president of Chase Manhattan Bank,
Ms. Linda Gotrocks. "Going down to the lab
to pick up my new baby."
　"A he or a she?" asks her secretary.
　"Oh, a he this time."
　　　　　　　　　　　　Office conversation, 1985

Fertilization of human eggs in the laboratory has already been accomplished by three separate scientific groups: Cambridge University physiologist Robert G. Edwards and gynecologist Patrick C. Steptoe are currently researching the implantation of artificially grown embryos in the wombs of women unable to conceive normally; embryo *transplants* in animals have been accomplished at Columbia-Presbyterian Medical Center.

If some women can have sex without pregnancy, and other women can have pregnancy without sex—or if the same woman can have either choice at different times—then the moral codes based on the axiom of sex equals pregnancy are as obsolete as witchcraft laws.

The transfer of human pregnancy to artificial wombs (which Aldous Huxley, in *Brave New World,* placed 500 years in the future) can't be more than ten or fifteen years away. General applications will inevitably follow, first for women who can't bear children, and then for women who want children but don't want nine months of discomfort and time lost from careers. The Hallmark card people will probably encourage the next generation to send Mother's Day cards to Johns Hopkins or Walter Reed with verses such as: "Put them all together, they spell OBSTETRICS/The ward that means the world to me."

When pregnancy is entirely separated from the human body, all that will remain of the purpose of sexual intercourse is love and delight; the old insistence that sex shouldn't be fun, or that it should be more than fun, will sound even sillier than the claim that there are cosmic moral dimensions in a football game.

> *"I'll have a few inches more height this year, Sam. The board has given me an executive post on Mars, and executives have to be dominant, you know. And I'd like a 12-inch penis; competition for women is fierce out there. Blue eyes, I guess. Trim down the waist a little."*
>
> Instructions from a businessman
> to his biotailor in the future

Artificial fertilization is only part of what Gordon Rattray Taylor characterized as *The Biological Time Bomb*. The bigger part is the concept of genetic engineering, which can be practically defined as the science of redesigning humanity to become anything it wants to become. As Nobel laureate Joshua Lederberg puts it, "The ultimate application of molecular biology would be the direct control of nucleotide sequences . . . to regulate, for example, the size of the human brain by prenatal or postnatal intervention." When pregnancy regularly occurs outside the female body and inside the laboratory, such interventions will become common.

Some molecular biologists already have carried the concept of genetic engineering to the point of seeking physical *immortality* in this generation. Dr. Paul Segall of the University of California at Berkeley, for instance, has invested 17 years in a search for the formula to reverse aging, and reports success with laboratory animals. Dr. José Froimovich, president of the Chilean Society of Gerontology and 11-time nominee for the Nobel prize in medicine, has also announced a major breakthrough "in the fight against aging," and Dr. Johan Bjorksten is working on a formula that he says might raise average life expectancy to a minimum of 150 years. Dr. Timothy Leary, always the bard of the avant minority in science, argues plausibly that if we mount a national campaign similar to the atomic Manhattan Project of the Forties or the space race of the Sixties, we can have immortality before 1990.

Another brave futurist, Dr. Isaac Asimov, points out in *The Genetic Code* that there seems to be a basic 60-year cycle between an intellectual breakthrough in the sciences and a total transformation of society by the new technology it unleashes. For instance, Edison noted electronic energy in 1883; 60 years later, electronic technology was phasing out electric technology, radar had helped win the war, and TV had been perfected (although not yet on the market). Similarly, Robert H. Goddard fired his first rocket into the air in 1926, and 60 years later, in 1986, we will be well along in the exploration of the local planets. As Asimov concludes, since DNA was identified in 1944, genetic technology should have revolutionized society by 2004; 1974 was the midpoint of that cycle, and the applications should be raining on us every year from now on. Note the heated debate about recombinant DNA research.

At a minimum, genetic engineering will produce newborn humans within 30 years who will be a quantum leap ahead of modern humanity (which already has a life span *30 years longer* than the average in 1840 England). As F. M. Esfandiary baldly proclaims in his *Up-Wingers,* "A Futurist Manifesto," "Today, when we speak of immortality and of going to another world, we no longer mean these in a theological or metaphysical sense. People are now striving for physical immortality. People are now traveling to other worlds. Transcendence has become a reality."

"Oh, baby, that was fantastic. I felt as
though I came for hours."
"You did—just under twenty hours, in fact."
Postcoital intimacies of the near future

Another trait of tomorrow's lovers will be their ability to turn on at will—with a little help from their chemical friends. Nathan S. Kline, M.D., says in *Psychotropic Drugs in the Year 2000* that we can expect real and specific aphrodisiacs by that date, as well as drugs that "foster or terminate mothering impulses." "Good Mommy" drugs, increasing maternal behavior, will no doubt be joyously endorsed by gentry like Billy Graham and widely prescribed by doctors and psychiatrists grappling with the housewife syndrome; but the latter group, terminating the whole mothering program, will be seized upon by dedicated career women and, if outlawed by establishment pressures, will be bootlegged by women's lib groups.

And this is only the new stuff. Many currently popular counterculture drugs are, if not real and specific aphrodisiacs, certainly powerful enhancers of sexuality, and they will not disappear—despite witch-hunts, secret-police tactics, midnight raids, and a general reign of terror against users. They will remain and become a larger part of the general public's ecstasy arsenal. As Ram Dass has testified: "Tim [Leary] is absolutely right about LSD enhancing sex. Before taking LSD, I never stayed in a state of sexual ecstasy for hours on end, but I have done this under LSD. It heightens all of your senses, and it means that you're living the sexual experience totally."

One of the interviewees in Barbara Lewis' *The Sexual Powers of Marihuana* testifies to curing herself of frigidity by use of the devil weed: "We turned on, and I can tell you, I've never been so turned on in my life. I was *really* turned on...."

We spent two hours at loveplay, the most intense loveplay, just letting it happen. . . . Finally, I went out of control—my facial muscles were twitching. My arms began to tingle . . . like it was just too much, as if I would explode. I just couldn't stand it. Then, when he got on top of me and we started fucking, I knew that it was going to happen and that nothing could stop it. It sounds silly, but I felt out in the universe . . . and I saw myself out there surrounded by stars."

Drugs that are either safer or less likely to spook the herd than grass, coke, and acid are certainly on the way. Dr. Kline predicts that by 2000 we will have drugs to control, reverse, accelerate, or extinguish virtually any emotion or compulsion. Ketamine (researched by Dr. John C. Lilly and allegedly given to astronauts to prepare them for zero gravity) seems to detach brain from body (and from body emotions) and leave one suspended in the yogic samadhi state for an hour at a time, as compared with the brief seconds of samadhi at LSD peak.

> "Hey, man, I've got some Einstein RNA—perfect for that physics exam you've got coming up. Only barter, no money. I'm looking for X-adrenaline for the track meet. Can you score it for me?"
>
> "Well, I've got some tryptophan—the stuff that stops time—and there's a guy in the Philosophy department who's always trying to score more of that. I'll see if he knows where X-adrenaline is being dealt."
>
> Two technology junkies doing business, 1990

Biofeedback promises even more than biochemicals—especially since Americans are not as paranoid about machines as they are about chemicals. Brain-wave research has already shown how to program oneself for the alpha, beta, theta, and delta states, which makes about 50 percent of the traditional yoga blissouts readily available to us today in somewhat less than two weeks—compared with anywhere from one to several years of orthodox hatha-yoga training. Continuation of this research can be expected to yield precise control of sexual-peak states (along with other desirable neural states) within a decade.

In fact, in 1976 a major breakthrough in sexual biofeedback was announced by Rutgers Medical School in New Jersey and Harvard University in Massachusetts, involving research in which male subjects tried to control the allegedly involuntary function of erection, with and without biofeedback. The group using biofeedback showed a 60 percent increase in voluntary control, while the other group showed only 10 percent. In related research, biofeedback has helped a subject—previously homosexual and then totally asexual as a result of crude behavior-modification techniques—to once again develop normal sexual functioning and to use it heterosexually.

Projecting such voluntary control over previously involuntary sexual functions only one or two decades into the future, one can easily see how the feats of tantric yoga or such LSD specialists as Dr. Leary and Ram Dass—e.g., staying in sexual ecstasy for hours on end—will be possible to anyone with a few weeks' training in biofeedback.

> *"Oh, darling, remember the night we met—the stars, the music and . . . us? I'd give anything to be back there again."*
> *"Hold on, while I plug you in."*
> 50th wedding anniversary conversation, 2001

Meanwhile, ESB—trade jargon for electrical stimulation of the brain—is opening as many neural doors as psychedelics and biofeedback combined. In one famous ESB experiment, a group of rats became so turned on by pressing a button that sent currents into the pleasure center of their brains that they starved to death, ignoring the food button in order to go on pleasuring themselves. In another test, an enraged bull was stopped in midcharge by an ESB wave activated by Yale physiologist J. M. R. Delgado.

Dr. Delgado has more recently specialized in retrieval of sensation by ESB. From his reports, it appears as if the sexual gourmets of 1990 not only will have aphrodisiacs to intensify pleasure, biofeedback training to control the previously involuntary functions (thereby abolishing frigidity, impotence, and premature ejaculation), and freedom from worry about unwanted pregnancies, but will also be able to reexperience any particular sexual sensation *at will.*

It staggers the mind to project what future sexologists will accomplish when they learn to combine the Masters and Johnson retraining techniques with biofeedback, neurochemicals such as LSD and ketamine, and ESB. Only those who already know such arcana as "A blow-job is ten times better with pot" or "Any orgasm is 50 times wilder with coke" will be able to imagine the sensual rebirth in store when, the taboos crumbling, science is able to frankly explore and teach the magnification and intensification of sexual experience. The prophet Blake will be vindicated: the whole creation will appear infinite and holy.

The "hedonic engineering" forecast by Dr. Timothy Leary will then become a reality. His general scenario for the outcome is as plausible as any and more likely than most: "[The future] will be scientific in essence and science fiction in style. . . . Politically, it will stress individualism, decentralization of authority, a live-and-let-live tolerance of difference, local option, and a mind-your-own-business libertarianism. . . . It will continue the trend toward open sexual expression and a more honest, realistic acceptance of both the equality and the magnetic difference between the sexes. . . . Advances in modern science now make it possible to develop an understanding of the nervous system, its evolution in the individual and the species, and the effects of chemical and electrical adjuvants on its expanding functions. . . . This understanding . . . is leading to a truly scientific philosophy of a self-responsible human nature." Tom Wolfe, who has already denounced the first stirrings of the Scientific Tantrism in violent terms, will go into paroxysms of rage, paranoia and envy when it reaches its full manifestation.

In other words, as we gain precise control over our nervous systems (a practical science that Leary calls neurologic), we will have less and less resemblance to the glandular-emotional robotism that the behaviorists found in studies of animals. Instead of being programmed and controlled by "involuntary" functions, we will program and control those functions ourselves. Then, at last, the alleged purpose of political democracy—"the pursuit of happiness"—will be more than a wistful phrase; it will become a practical goal.

The self-programming man or woman has no quarrel with deviates, heretics, and subcultures of bizarre belief, so long as they in turn remain nonviolent and noncoercive. This is why those with the greatest joy in life—the economically secure aristocracies, the artsy-craftsy drop-out groups who accept poverty as the price of freedom—have always had the greatest tolerance for sexual (and other) heretics. As general misery decreases and self-programming skill increases, a similar tolerance will spread into all segments of society. The quarrel between the *Playboy* bachelor and the women's lib careerist, or between the hetero and the gay, will seem as absurd as the War of the Roses or the feud between Big-endians and Little-endians in *Gulliver's Travels.*

The loose tolerance introduced by such overtouted and imperfect systems as psychoanalysis and behavior modification will escalate into real tolerance when true neurologic and hedonic engineering are unleashed in the next decade or two. Norman O. Brown's visionary version of Freud's "polymorphous perversity" (total sensory turn on) will inevitably follow.

> *"Hi, I'm Joe and this is my substitute, ACE-IV."*
> *"Gee, he's cute."*
> Singles' bar come-on of the Eighties

The vibrator—first as shady joke, then a growing fad—has already prepared us for the technologization of sex, so introduction of the artificial sex partner will come as little surprise. Rudimentary doll-like models are already for sale; one (called the *Deep Throat* model, naturally) is even capable of performing fairly realistic fellatio. Hedy Lamarr's autobiography, *Ecstasy and Me,* reveals that a former lover of hers had a very elaborate imitation Hedy manufactured to give him solace when their affair went on the rocks. Such developments indicate that in sex, as elsewhere, desire plus money equals results—or, as George S. Kaufman once said of a friend's new estate, "This is what God could have done, if He'd had the money."

Are we talking about substitute sex for the crippled, the malformed, the hopelessly ugly or neurotic? Only in the first generation of such technology. Brain-wave and other biofeedback studies lead inevitably into the concept of cybernetic sex robots programmed to scan neural signals from the human partner and provide exactly, precisely, exquisitely what is desired in every second of sexual union. In fact, reports from Masters and Johnson indicate that their crude and precybernetic (brainless) ACE model (artificial coital equipment) produced no frustration in the women who tried it. Eventually such mechanized substitutes can be programmed for an effect "better than the real thing," as William S. Burroughs fantasized in his Sixties science fiction novel *The Soft Machine.*

In recent years, Johns Hopkins Applied Physics Laboratory in Baltimore possessed a 100-pound robot, affectionately dubbed The Beast, that knows how to "feed" itself; i.e., to seek electric outlets and recharge its circuits when its power runs low. Sim One, an experimental robot at University of Southern California, has the external features of a man, stands over six feet tall and has a normal pulse rate, blood pressure, and heartbeat; is white-skin-colored, moves its diaphragm and chest in simulation of breathing, and even possesses a tongue, teeth, and vocal cords. Sim's keepers plan improved models that will sweat, bleed, cry out in pain and eventually replace cadavers in training medical students. The Sim One of today combined with the Masters and Johnson ACE of today would already constitute a crude artificial playmate for women. A more complete Hedy Lamarr doll (or Linda Lovelace, or Raquel Welch) cannot be far away.

> *"Wonder why Smith 23X hasn't come out of his house in the past week? And what are all those buzzing and humming mechanical noises?"*
> *"I dunno. But a truck marked Artificial Paradise made a big delivery there last Thursday."*
> Back-fence gossip, circa 1985

Yes: why not a totally programmed sexual environment? Saul Kent, who has described this concept as "multimedia masturbation," envisions sex tapes for the house computer, programmed for the ideal all-around sexual trip—with or without partner. Already, X-rated motels in California provide water beds and closed-circuit TV featuring porn films, so that a shy couple can have a simulated orgy and share their real selves with each other and the images of Georgina Spelvin, Harry Reems, and Marilyn Chambers. The next step, easily obtainable for the rich even now, is to program the whole inner environment of the bedroom for a fantasy that goes well with the sex act. ESB control of brain centers via this computer-programmed artificial environment would give, in Burroughs' perfect phrase, "precise control over thought, feeling, and *apparent* sensory impression" (italics his). Reality in that room would be whatever you wanted it to be.

Of course, in a sense we already live inside that room, as the Buddhists know. That is, the human nervous system, properly programmed, can edit and orchestrate all experience into any gestalt it wishes. We encounter the same dismal and depressing experiences over and over because they are repeating tape loops in the central programmer of our brains. We can encounter ecstasy over and over by learning the neurosciences that orchestrate all incoming signals into ecstatic tape loops. *The contact has already happened right where you are sitting now.* Whether it is tuned-in or not-tuned-in depends on your skill as metaprogrammer.

Multimedia pornography will enthrall millions when it first appears; porn light shows, porn 3-D, and porn holograms are the dawning intimations of a revolution that will climax—certainly by the early years of the next century—when the difference between porn and the artificial sex mate will no longer be visible: multimedia solipsism and all-channel masturbation will be the pleasure norms.

Such a sensory revolution would amount to the creation of a fifth brain, or neurosomatic brain, according to Dr. Leary, who contends that we already have four: a survival-program brain, an emotional-territory brain, a symbolic-logic brain, and a sex-bonding brain. The new neurosomatic brain will give us eventual total control of sensation for a state of rapture. Yogis, shamans, and modern research subjects in sensory deprivation (i.e., environmental monotony) turn on this fifth brain, at least temporarily, and forever after rave about the *pure bliss* they have experienced—the sheer godliness of it all: "I AM who AM." "I have become God," wrote Baudelaire, the French poet, and he was under the influence of only a single crude neurochemical (hashish) and never knew the effects of the biofeedback and brain-wave technology currently dawning.

There is also, according to Dr. Leary, a potential sixth brain in which "neurophysical transformations can be accomplished"—the kind of macroscopic quantum jumping our ancestors called magic or sorcery; a potential seventh brain containing the "neurogenetic archives," which will allow us to tap the DNA/RNA dialog and to consciously recall all incidents in evolution and all lessons previously kept on autopilot (the unconscious), thus making us consciously 3.5 billion years old and consciously immortal; and a potential eighth brain, or metaphysiological circuit, linking us to all other high intelligences in the galaxy. This last has also been reported by Dr. Lilly in his *Simulations of God.*

Another road to godmanship is mapped by physicist R. C. W. Ettinger, who started the immortalist (called, more properly, cryonics) movement of the Sixties with the utopian slogan "Freeze—wait—reanimate!" Professor Ettinger argues, in *Man into Superman* (1972), that after molecular biology really gets into high gear, "the sexual superwoman may be riddled with cleverly designed orifices of various kinds, something like a wriggly Swiss cheese, but shapelier and more fragrant; and her supermate may sprout assorted protuberances, so that they intertwine and roll over each other in a million permutations of The Act, tireless as hydraulic pumps. . . . A perpetual grapple, no holes barred, could produce a continuous state of multiple orgasm."

It will be noted that Professor Ettinger gets to the same projected destination (ecstatic mind) by a totally different line of scientific projection. Most of the bright-eyed young guys in molecular biochemistry these days have their own personal roadmaps to that destination. A physicist with whom I once participated in a radio discussion of futurism even has a plan for mankind to achieve ecstatic immortality by becoming *lasers.*

A significant—though subtle—part of this sexual transformation of humanity has already occurred in the Western world. Few realize today that the church fathers' horrible anal metaphors for sex (stinking, filthy, putrid, etc.) were literally accurate until modern medicine and the development of *soap* made bodily sweetness accessible to more than the very rich. As Aldous Huxley points out in his *Tomorrow and Tomorrow and Tomorrow*, these puritanical putdowns of the body as well as the old aristocratic sneers at "the stinking masses" were quite natural to the fastidious of those days. R. Buckminster Fuller remarks in his *Utopia or Oblivion* that members of the average workingman's family in 1905—when Fuller's family first moved to Carbondale, Illinois—were foul-smelling, toothless, and ready for death at age 42.

The sexual revolution, like the world's political-economic revolutions, stems from the discovery that people *don't have to* remain foul, and the future shock of our time is due entirely to the acceleration of technology, since theological and political terrorists have not been able to punish researchers (except for non-Lamarckian geneticists in Russia and psychedelic therapists in the USA).

> *"Sylvia, will you marry me?"*
> *"Yes, but we'll have to wait—I'm going male for the next couple of months, to do research for my new tape novel."*
> Two lovers, circa 2025

Peeking further into the mid-distance—early in the next century—the rise of life expectancy to 500 years (the goal for which biologist Paul Segall is aiming right now) will probably make sex-change operations fashionable for many who are not psychological transsexuals in the traditional sense. Rather, many will want to become the opposite sex temporarily for such purposes as (1) curiosity—scientific, sexual, or otherwise; (2) "personal growth," i.e., the artistic, literary, or philosophical stimulation; or (3) entering a new extraplanetary environment where either the small, tough, long-lived female body or the large-muscled, quickly aggressive male body might be decidedly advantageous over the other.

A great deal of the erotic realism of such writers as Joyce, D. H. Lawrence, and even, at times, Hemingway, is an attempt to get inside the female mind and see men—in the sex act and in other relationships—as women see them. Presumably, many gynecologists and obstetricians share empathetically in the female functions they tend to, and many an artist has decidedly fused into the glorious nude female models he paints. The desire to become the opposite sex for a while is also evident in women's writings, especially women's lib tracts. Sex change in the future will not be restricted to compulsive people.

> *"She's wearing see-through shoes—must be*
> *a foot fetishist, too."*
> Street comment of the next decade

Buckminster Fuller and Robert Heinlein, among other futurists, have predicted that clothes will be phased out as temperature and climate control are realized. My own hunch is that nudity will be everywhere (already many California beaches are as casual as Denmark's), but that clothes will also be everywhere; the difference will be that clothes will serve primarily as sexual signaling devices, which, according to one school of anthropology, was their original function.

Kubrick's joke in *A Clockwork Orange*, imagining a revival of the Renaissance codpiece, or enlarged peter-heater, may be a quite accurate prediction. Similar decorations for the female breasts already exist in porn and in other entertainment, and may soon escape into the streets. The old homosexual code—green on Thursdays—may be flooded in an ocean of similar sartorial signals as S/M people, exhibitionists, and other erotic minorities go public.

> *"I didn't get any last night—my clone had a*
> *headache."*
> Locker-room lament of the year 2000

If eugenists' dreams are to soon come true, so then will some of their nightmares. As hundreds of Albert Schweitzers and Albert Einsteins are reproduced in the laboratories when genetic roulette has a fixed wheel, then the public, having other interests besides humanism and science, will demand and get real-life duplicates of contemporary Mick Jaggers and Marilyn Monroes.

The Mick Jagger of 2005, in fact, will probably graduate from millionaire to billionaire by selling clones of himself out of which millions of Mick Jaggers will be mass-produced for all the lustful lads and lassies who dig the real Mick Jagger. Why not? Any guy today can already have Norma Jean the Angel Child just by closing his eyes. A millionaire with a cosmetic surgeon and a female subject possessing (to start with) 70 percent of the basic physical equipment can have her with his eyes open.

> *"Are you still hung up on that Sophia Loren*
> *gyndroid? Let me show you how to tune your*
> *brain waves into this euphometer and focus*
> *into perpetual ecstasy. . . ."*
> Evil social influence, 2025

Could sex, after achieving its full flowering, wither away entirely? Is the true future of sex no sex at all? When reproduction is confined to the laboratory and sex has only the function of pleasure communication, it may well develop that even the most intensified sex cannot compete with generalized neural pleasure. This may or may not define eternal masturbation, depending on how strictly one identifies sex with genitalia.

Herbert Marcuse predicts, in *Eros and Civilization*, that such a hedonic technology will retool the human nervous system in the same general direction of continual rapture foreseen in Norman O. Brown's *Love's Body*. (Some adepts of yoga and LSD claim to have achieved this already.) It is striking that the Dionysian visions of Brown and Marcuse, based entirely on Freud's analysis of what the unconscious mind really *wants*, are quite similar to the consensus of futurist probes into what the oncoming biotechnology can deliver. This can hardly be coincidence. Evidently, we have always sought our deepest yearnings, though consciously only daring to express them as myths or fantasies, while pretending to ourselves that we were accepting the grim, pessimistic, hardnosed view of the hurt-child aspect of ourselves.

Commenting on Dr. Otto Fenichel's observation that "behind every form of play lies a process of discharge of masturbatory fantasies," Brown says: "Nothing wrong, except [Fenichel's] refusal to play: when our eyes are opened to the symbolic meaning, our only refuge is loss of shame, polymorphous perversity, pansexualism; penises everywhere. As in tantric yoga, in which any sexual act may become a form of mystic meditation, and any mystic state may be interpreted sexually."

The civilization of polymorphous perversity forecast by Brown, the society without repression described by Marcuse, the hedonic engineering of Leary, are dawning, and those who think I've been writing about our children or grandchildren are mistaken. If star flight and immortality arrive when some futurists expect (1990 to 2010), then, even as the last of the anxiety-ridden terrestrial mortals are reading and rejecting this chapter, some of the first of the ecstatic cosmic immortals are also reading it and accepting it.

BY SUMMARY OF WAY

A few may get through the gate in time.
William S. Burroughs,
Cities of the Red Night

"General Haig raised his beef for glory . . ."

"And for riches, they are not long . . ."

"Creatures lacking the gate, you fair-haired sons of bitches!"

"The weeping and the laughter *has sentenced you to die!*"

"Six million people fast forward . . ."

"They are not long and *the process* is continuing."

One day Jesus had finished healing several thousand people and wanted to rest, but just then a hundred lepers came over a nearby hill looking for him. Quickly, Jesus said to a disciple, "Man, I'm beat. Let me duck into that tent, and you go meet those lepers and cure them."

The disciple, Luke, protested, "But I'm only an ordinary physician. What do I know about faith-healing?"

Looking him straight in the eye, Jesus said,

"Use the Force, Luke!"

Which is from the selected writings of Ed Zdrojewski, on the other side. Parmenides' World II, the timeless realm—beyond the Gutenberg fix—Castaneda's *nagual*—Parsifal could only find it *after* passing through Chapel Perilous, dig?

Till we have built Jerusalem in Reagan's grim unpleasant land . . . "I'm only an ordinary machine to bring you a thunderbolt . . . This stage of libidinal development brought a boy back in mini-skirts . . .

Penis raised his beef as typified by Henry Ford—April 23, 1014 at Clontarf, the X factor that triggers an ordinary physician . . . junkyard cyanide . . .

Pisa, in the 23rd year of the mind—I was close to the Apaches, i.e., the food supply—nor shall the diamond die into its talkative seven politics—the Space Freaks, who may or may not be infiltrated—I don't know how humanity repeating the same God—girdle advertisements, Hitler's last secret weapon—*politics by normal means eats those who create it*—

There was another America dark petals of iron—

Voices crying out for peace

"Gentlepersons," said Clem Cotex, "I think we are living in a novel."

There were no ladies present, but Clem had been barked at and snarled at so often for saying "gentlemen" that he had been conditioned to use the genderless form. On his planet, the domesticated primates maintain pack-taboos by barking and snarling at those who violate the semantic grids that control thoughts, feeling and (apparent) sense impressions.

The members of the Warren Belch Society shifted uneasily in their chairs; Blake Williams, the anthropologist, in trying to stifle a yawn accidentally released a belch.

"Um yes we are familiar with your fondness for that um er metaphor," Dr. Williams said quickly, trying to cover the belch that had covered the yawn that had covered his boredom with his whole inane subject.

"It's not a metaphor," Clem protested immediately.

"All that is, is metaphor," Simon Moon quoted. "Fossil poetry. It runs on controlled explosions."

"The work of our Society," Cotex reminded them, "is to investigate theories so wild that most people won't even think about them. I insist that my theory is wild enough to qualify."

"You've said all this before," Simon said. "And we have thought about it. It's a good metaphor, as Dr. Williams says, but that's all it is: a metaphor."

"Gentlepersons," Clem plowed on, "we have never yet seriously considered the nature of the Novelist."

"Oh, Jesus," Professor Fred ("Fidgets") Digits muttered, at the other end of the table.

"I don't like this metaphor," Dr. Horace Naismith said. "I don't think there is a Novelist. I think we are emerging from some random word generator—some of these bits concern a coolant failure—connecting and reconnecting—"

Clem Cotex shook his head stubbornly. "Webster does not play dice with the language," he said. "If I see motion, I deduce a motor. The Novelist is the motor. He or She . . ."

"Why not It?" Simon Moon asked innocently.

"He or She," Clem plowed on, not ready to deal with that one, "has created our thoughts, feelings and (apparent) sense impressions. We exist only in the Mind of the Novelist, as pure concepts, and therefore we are infinitely permutable. We can all be changed in an instant, in the blinking of an eye. We are not the form but the form-making capacity, dig?"

"You mean," Simon Moon objected, "because we are parts of the Novelist, we are not *things*. That's kinda like the implicate wholeness in David Bohm's interpretation of quantum mechanics. The Mind of the Novelist is the whole; each seeming 'event' in our lives is just an *eigenstate* . . ."

"A variable," Clem said quickly. "*Eigenstates* are made up of the superposition of state vectors, which are the basic metaphors of the poem of quantum physics . . ."

"Jeez-*us*," Fred Digits moaned. "What have you been smoking lately? That new sinsemilla from Mendocino?"

"When he tells us to worship the Novelist," Dr. Williams said ironically, "I'll know our Society is evolving into a new church of some sort . . ."

"No, no, no!" Clem's protest was vehement. "The Novelist is our enemy!"

The TV in the next room: *"The President has not been hit . . . The 23-year-old assailant from Colorado . . ."*

"I'd just like to go back to the '20s."

"The dirty rats running a whorehouse."

On March 28, 1979, something began to go wrong. Whyfor had they, it is Hiberio-Miletians and Argloe-Noremen during the first three minutes. We operate here by the precisely calculated birth of an otion.

And what of Himana, that their tolvtubular high fidelity Ecology, or hip neo-puritanism, as modern as tomorrow afternoon and in appearance running a whorehouse.

The TV again· *"The President walked into the hospital . . . the 22-year-old assailant . . ."*

And they still make jokes about it:

"What gives milk and glows in the dark?"

"A cow anywhere near Three Mile Island."

Vacaville Prison, 1973: I am rapping with Dr. Timothy Leary (in for poor usage of the First Amendment) and David Hilliard (in for assaulting an officer of the law). We are discussing Eldridge Cleaver, who is not universally admired in this group. Hilliard, a former Black Panther, speaks with profound resignation, passing weary judgment on Cleaver, on himself, on the world, on the Empire:

"Man, we've all got the Oppressor *inside.*"

But Mallarmé, on the other hand, defines the function of poetry as "to purify the dialect of the tribe."

We have come to bring you metaphors:

The *Grundgestalt* is everywhere present, like Bohm's Hidden Variable; in the *Appassionata* (Sonata 23) it begins with the initial Neapolitan theme, or maybe after sniffing too much glue. Pull me out, I am half convinced that precise mathematical equations will eventually be written, as in Hesse's *Bead Game,* because in essence Beethoven was even more analytical than Bach. The sonata is a series of theorems logically deduced from the (unstated) *Grundgestalt,* vaguely Neapolitan. Shannon calls it the manifestation of a Markoff Chain.

"Mean sonofabitch kinda dog, add that to the stew."

"Look out, mama. You can't beat him."

"The enormous tragedy of the optimistic, despite the machinations of the wicked . . ."

Liddy said that Mitchell told him Greenspun becomes a functional process, a relationship between the motions of blackmail type material.

Whish! A firecracker went off.

"The Damned Thing which couldn't exist."

"Police . . . Mama . . . Helen . . . Mother . . . Please take me out."

On December 8, 1972, United Airlines Flight 553 remains optimistic, despite the machinations of the definite *chicken.*

"Manes was so much like a Taco."

Liddy said, "We have come to bring you bean soup."

There is no other place.

"Some brothers call this the motion of blackmail."

"They won't let *me* get purple in hashish clarity."

"Come on, open the soap duckets."

The only way I can account for this wild idea is a private burglary for Howard Hughes.

A revolutionary new concept in art Under Attack:

Logic is in trouble, too. Brouwer denied the universality of the Law of the Excluded Middle (which holds that the universe is either A or not-A, with no maybe). Tarski produced a multi-valued logic, including a *maybe.* Anatole Rapoport has proposed a four-valued logic including the true, the false, the indeterminate, and the meaningless. G. Spencer Brown has a three-valued logic (true, false and imaginary) which has been successfully applied to computers and biological systems.

"In a whirlwind, the infant Hitler . . ."

"Some of them never went authoritarian."

Being very careful to get a good grip with each leg, then I found the apartment house.

Thus, we have four logics, four definitions of proof, four geometries, six quantum theories, two ways of understanding General Relativity, and a hundred years of social science that demonstrates that any model of the universe will make sense eventually if we share space-time and conversation with people who believe in that model.

"Hold on. We have come to bring you black men, blue men . . ."

F A S T   F O R W A R D

"We have reached the watershed. The 80s will be a period seen in retrospect as either one of extraordinary creativity or a period when the international order literally came apart—politically, economically and morally."

Source: Willy Brandt, *Future Abstracts,* 1980

$$2 \times 2 \times$$
$$E = mc^2$$

MATT GOLUB 82

CREDO

A god is a metaphor that illuminates existence.

No man and no woman is yet wise enough to say if such metaphors are invented or discovered. We know only that they illuminate us by beauty, by power, by coherence.

Beauty is not sufficient to manifest a living god, a metaphor that illuminates us. Beauty manifests nymphs and sirens and various elementals; but a god is known also by power and coherence.

Power, similarly, may not manifest a living god. Power manifests demons and satyrs and monsters; but a god is known also by beauty and coherence.

Coherence, in like fashion, may not manifest a living god. Coherence manifests temples in which gods may dwell. These temples need not be architectural in the strict sense; Bach's music, the multiplication table, the Tarot cards, the Periodic Table of Elements, great paintings, and many similar artifacts, are temples in which a living god may dwell.

One knows that a god is in the temple when, after contemplating the coherence of the structure, one is seized, violently, by the power and beauty of it, as by a light or a flame or an effulgence.

This illumination is a discharge of compressed energy and information.

A god may be present in a temple for one viewer and not for another. This is a common occurrence, because men and women are various, and differ in their capacity to apprehend beauty and power and coherence.

One may learn to apprehend beauty more fully; this is the function of the arts.

One may learn to apprehend power more fully; this is the function of technology.

One may learn to apprehend coherence more fully; this is the function of pure science and philosophy.

Those who apprehend beauty only are said to be seduced by the nymphs or sirens. The Irish say that "their minds have been stolen by the faeries."

Those who apprehend power only become possessed by demons, and they are figuratively said to give birth to monsters.

Those who apprehend coherence only become empty shells and mausoleums, ruins and labyrinths.

One may understand a god partially or fully.

Those who understand gods partially may think of them as linguistic constructs, or information systems, or psychological complexes, or historical laws, or in other partial ways.

To understand a god fully is to become one with the god. This cannot be achieved without balance.

It is far easier to become one with a nymph, an elemental, a demon, a monster or an empty mausoleum.

All mystics of all traditions agree that a god may not be exploited.

Organized religions are conspiracies to exploit various gods, by flattering them, by compelling them through ritual, or by bribing them. Experience indicates that these techniques do not work, and the would-be exploiters are merely seduced by sirens or possessed by demons or otherwise become themselves the exploited.

A god is not shown or manifest, a theophany does not occur, until exploitation is abandoned for simple love. There may be beauty and power and coherence, but the god is only apprehended dimly, not comprehended fully, until the mind is enflamed by love.

This is the meaning of Spinoza's remark that "the intellectual love of things consists of understanding their perfections"; and of Richard St. Victor's *"Amare videre est"* (To love is to perceive).

A god is known *by* beauty and power and coherence, but a god is only known *through* love. This is the essence of the mystics' saying, "The door opens inward."

It is possible, and even probable, that nymphs and satyrs and such are only gods who have been apprehended without love—partially, obscurely, distortedly.

I believe in Bach, the creator of heaven and earth, and in Mozart, his only begotten son, and in Beethoven the mediator and comforter; and inasmuch as their gods have manifested also in Vivaldi and Ravel and Stravinsky and many another, I believe in the communion of saints, the forgiveness of error, and Mind everlasting.

I believe in Leonardo, the creator of heaven and earth, and in Michelangelo, his only begotten son, and in Raphael the mediator and comforter; and inasmuch as their gods have manifested also in Rubens and Van Gogh and Picasso and many another, I believe in the communion of saints, the forgiveness of error, and Mind everlasting.

I believe in Newton, the creator of heaven and earth, and in Maxwell, his only begotten son, and in Einstein the mediator and comforter; and inasmuch as their gods have manifested also in Schrödinger and Heisenberg and Bohr and many another, I believe in the communion of saints, the forgiveness of error, and Mind everlasting.

All gods are quite mortal, and yet immortal. They are betrayed and condemned and destroyed, and *it must be so;* but they live again, in more subtle forms. This is the meaning of Resurrection, and of Reincarnation, and of Progress; it is the meaning, too, of the Rosicrucian motto: *"Ex Deo nascimur, in Jesu mortimur, per spiritum sanctum reviviscimus."* (From God we are born, in Jesus we die, by the Holy Spirit we live again.)

There are gods many, as there are beauties and powers and coherences of various orders, but they culminate in unity.

Where there is no love, the gods do not disappear; but they are apprehended grotesquely, as contraptions or automatons.

All forms of Determinism are based on misapprehending the gods as contraptions or automatons.

The gods are liberators, because they manifest the power of Mind over contraptions and automatons.

A god, a metaphor that prevails, contains information but radiates energy; which is why one cannot separate language from Mind, or poetry from being.

SUMMARY OF BY WAY

*Apollonius of Tyana, writing as Hermes
Trismegistos, said, "That which is above
is that which is below." By this he meant
to tell us that our universe is a hologram,
but he lacked the term.*

Valis, Philip K. Dick

Phil Dick wasn't the only one to think our experience
is a hologram. That is also the opinion of neurologist Karl
Pribram and physicist David Bohm.

The amusing thing about a hologram is that the information of the whole is in any part, as in Schoenberg's *Grundgestalt* concept of music. You can take a hologram as big as
Africa, chop out one square inch, and that piece contains all
the information of the Africa-sized piece. Or you can take a
hologram as big as the universe, take out one atom, and you
still have all the in-form-ation of the universe . . . if you know
how to read it.

"Then information is the Hidden Variable . . ."

The Empire has sentenced you to die. It's that simple, if
you want it in lean unlovely English. "Nobody is entitled to
anything." Got it? The Grail is, always has been, and cannot
be anything else but, Immortality.

They do not want you thinking about coming unstuck
in time.

"99 and 44/100 percent pure Marilyn Chambers to
double to two jesuses," Einstein calculated.

"Is that the whole difference or Jehovah walking
around?" Mozart exclaimed.

It may be visualized as the giant ape, Kong.

"A monster unleashed or created by atomic radiation . . . pure Marilyn Chambers would never be painful."

"Worse yet, the monster is being produced by surviving Nazis!" Joe Malik shouted.

"The Hoovians never wept nor filled the white light." The walls between urinals left Washington and headed for Chicago. On board was Sgt. Joe Friday kind of glazed over. A potential sixth brain would never be created by atomic radiation. I have found no better chap in Canada.

"Arresting officer Sgt. Joe Friday spent two hours in loveplay, the most intense loveplay, in the 1920s. Karl Haushofer, Roy Rogers and his horse, Trigger, wish you could get my vibrator. Visionary experiences for the Insect Trust, *if enough people believe in them . . .*"

"Advances in modern science without balance?"

"Like some kind of invisible ray . . . visionary experience . . . to consider physics some kind of poem . . ."

"In 1944, when the war was proving to last longer . . . six million people are hooked into the emic reality . . . The awakening from robotism might suggest Krupp is an isolationist . . . This administration was busted and hauled off to jail . . ."

Those who control symbols, smart enough and bold enough to grab what we want.

"In the 1920s, Karl Haushofer following the physical sciences combined with the Masters-Johnson ACE is prepared to deal with change on such a scale."

"Scientists, like lesser mortals, are hooked into the emic reality."

"There was a picture of Jesus busted and hauled off to jail . . ."

"Marilyn Chambers will probably graduate from millionaire to billionaire, and some peaking!"

"Karl Haushofer . . . six million people later died . . ."

Dr. Williams almost dropped the pipe he was about to ignite. "Run that by me again," he said slowly.

"As ideas in the Novelist's Mind," Clem said, "we are potentially—no, actually—infinite. There is no limit to how far we can develop, if you follow me. But when He puts us in a novel, we become trapped in that system. We lose our infinite freedom and become de-*finite* laws of form . . ."

"You've been reading G. Spencer Brown on acid again," Simon Moon said accusingly.

"Sounds like Christian Science to me," added Dr. Naismith.

"No, wait," Blake Williams said thoughtfully. "I think Clem has hit on something . . . it's what the Gnostics were trying to say, in denying the reality of perceptions . . ."

"I say we emerge from pure chaos by stochastic processes . . ."

". . . from the Nuclear Regulatory Commission . . ."

"The Yippies surged forward like a 12-inch penis . . . the marauding bands of Grandma's illustrated Bible . . ."

The collapse of the state vector.

Boldly stealing from Roman Polansky, I call it Chinatown. This book is an Information Machine, connecting and reconnecting . . . meltdown . . . Junkyard Dog . . . omnidimensional halo . . . *Blue lions* in Berkeley.

THE CENTER IS EVERYWHERE. IT IS IMMEDIATELY AVAILABLE RIGHT WHERE YOU ARE SITTING NOW.

But A cannot contain A + B?

Then A must become A + B. This is the technical definition of Samadhi, the union of Self and Not-Self.

The Contactee is a medieval Irishman: "Asthma would be less painful . . ."

Time is in-form-ation.

Fuller simplifies Einstein into a one-sentence poem: "Matter is knots in energy."

Matter is interference patterns. All radiations travel in geodesics, due to gravity which curves their trajectories. Where these trajectories cross, interference results: knots in energy, perceived by us as "matter."

The world of matter is the tuned-in. The not-yet-tuned-in is not *not*, it is merely not *knot*. Dig?

Tim Leary asked, 1968:

"WHAT do you turn on when you turn on?"

Omatoes for dinner creates weird energy fluctuations. The function of This Department is to seek juxtaposition of idea and image, looking now through the McLuhanesque montage of the daily newspaper.

A visitor from your home country suddenly looks alien and images are a mechanism:

"Think of junk, garbage—any large city—rats—within the temples, Euclidean space—Chinatown in the dark . . ."

"The Jonestown Nazis . . . cyanide during *Illuminatus!* . . . Captain Whitehouse can read history . . ."

Dr. Williams said guardedly, "Then the Novelist must be part of some larger reality . . ."

"Exactly," Clem Cotex said vehemently. "He is playing at being God but he's only some kind of *demiurge* or *pan-urgia* . . ."

"My bleeding piles," Simon Moon protested. "This is nothing but First-Century Gnostic metaphysics . . ."

·The first man to enter outer space was very passionate and I could see that people in the audience were kind of glazed-over and the process is continuing . . ."

"Flight 553 stopped with the last estimate . . . words like witchcraft and Tantra and sex magick . . ."

"You must realize that you can go right at the whole picture to get some perspective . . ."

"Of course, we can't be certain . . . the French in Russia . . . Marilyn and abnormal brain functioning . . ."

"Geophysical shock waves in a late Beethoven symphony . . ."

This is the cage of "werewolf space." Mickey Mouse inversions. swamp gas by Rutgers Medical School. I'll bear it on me. To remind me in all directions . . .

At the opposite extreme is the Superdeterminist model of quantum mechanics as presented by Fritjof Capra, which denies "contrafactual definiteness," i.e., it denies that a statement about what could happen is a real statement. This is even more radical than it sounds. It means that I had no real choice about which random elements got into this book, And/Or Press had no choice about publishing it, and you had no choice about reading it at this point in time right where you are sitting now.

I call this the Slaughter Machine to bring you metaphors: Marilyn Chambers to blow Captain Whitehouse: definitions so much like a Taco.

In this regard, any associated supporting element is, of course, Garfinkle's star pupil, Carlos Castaneda, who talks to coyotes. That is, Castaneda describes the sorcerer's emic reality from *inside,* and presents extremely interesting challenges to the total system rationale.

Ethnomethodology seems to demonstrate that there are no axioms that can withstand persistent *breaching.* Social scientists can even be brought to doubt that they understand crime better than the criminal, insanity better than the lunatic, or sorcery better than the sorcerer.

But I am dying. The racketeers or national crime syndicate would have a collection to system compatibility testing. Can't do another thing. Look out, circumstantial possibilities of indefinite elaboration, right where you are sitting now.

Sometimes, I see across time and know things before they happen; that is the Sin of Precognition. Other times, I see across space and know things happening elsewhere; that is the Sin of Clairvoyance. I even, on some occasions, do not seem to be locked into euclidean space, and travel freely in many dimensions; that is the Sin of Astral Projection. For these crimes against the Empire, Rev. Dr. Carl Sagan of the First Church of Fundamentalist Materialism condemns me to nonentity. He says I am not real.

Energy in-forms matter as I in-form you when *any etic experience becomes emic culture.*

The product configuration baseline adds overriding red, white and blue cockroaches.

Wonderbread transplants have been accomplished.

Think of your desires as toilet tissue.

"Dr. Commoner said space cities and marauding bands of mountain lions . . ."

"The big gorilla was *strong* in hashish clarity."

Ezra Pound said, "Great, damn it. The flying saucer *is* the naked skin."

You got no trigger but beings from indefinite future.

"Police, police . . . dog biscuit . . . please keep him home . . ."

"Reserve decision in the universe."

Where these signals cross will predict a second signal. I don't know if that system would work. (The mystical bliss-out.) Skeletons in Naval uniforms: "Exploring Mexico, the sea and sexuality . . ."

There was another America crying out for peace . . .

The power to define a Junkyard Dog.

"No more muddy mess. It's no problem for a boy. But I am the Father of the Hydrogen Bomb."

Look out, mama. Several thousand Nazi soldiers have been mind-programmed.

Being very careful to get a good grip with each leg, then I found the apartment house.

"Hold on. We have come to bring you bean soup."

The walls between urinals left Washington and headed for Chicago. On board was Dorothy Hunt kind of glazed over. A potential sixth brain would never be created by atomic radiation.

Liddy spent two hours in loveplay, the most intense loveplay, in the 1920s. Karl Haushofer, Roy Rogers and his horse, Trigger, wish you could get my vibrator.

"The spirits quickly control symbols."

"In the streets . . . dog now . . ."

"Think of junk, garbage—any large city—rats—within the temples, Euclidean space—Chinatown in the dark . . ."

"And the clash of our cries for peace."

"Or say that stone is the speech."

"Space cities this morning, ours."

". . . prone to earthquakes and marauding bands of mountain lions . . ."

"I am passing a *chicken!*"

"The blue color for peace."

"So soft with space."

"Larger programming going on simultaneously."

"Do not murmer."

"Nor know."

"Nor the lions. For the Freudians."

"Many passages. Two more."

"Eight pieces to the utmost."

Contact has been made. The Junkyard Dog glares malevolently from rusted old Model-T Ford. "Let's win this one for the Gipper!"

We leap from human bodies. Fast forward.

GLOSSARY

EMIC REALITY The thoughts, feelings and (apparent) sense impressions that people create by talking to each other (or by communicating in any symbolism); the semantic environment.

ENERGY From the Greek, *en-ergia,* that which works. Energy can only do work when it is organized; the organizing principle is **INFORMATION** (see below).

ENTROPY The amount of disorder in a system; the reciprocal or reverse of the amount of information in a system.

ETHNOMETHODOLOGY The study of comparative emic realities; how symbolisms create our thoughts, feelings and (apparent) sense impressions.

ETIC REALITY The hypothetical reality that has not been filtered through a human nervous system. If you think you have anything to say about it, without using words, equations, or other brain-symbolism, please send a complete description to the author.

GENERAL SEMANTICS The brand of **NEUROSEMAN-TICS** invented by Count Alfred Korzybski; see **NEURO-SEMANTICS.**

HIDDEN VARIABLES The unknowns beyond space-time which create everything we perceive within space-time; the information that organizes energy. A concept from the physics of David Bohm.

IMPLICATE ORDER The realm of the Hidden Variables, in Dr. Bohm's quantum physics.

INFORMATION The self-organizing principles that causes a system to become more coherent; mathematically, the reverse of the probability that you can predict what the system will transmit next. Also called "negative entropy" by computer scientists, or "syntropy" by Buckminster Fuller.

NEGATIVE ENTROPY The amount of coherence in a system.

NEUROSEMANTICS The study of how semantics affects the nervous system; how the local reality-labyrinth programs our thoughts, feelings and (apparent) sense impressions.

NOÖSPHERE The expanding omnidimensional structure of all reality-labyrinths on this planet; the sum total of all human thoughts, feelings and (apparent) sense impressions. A term from the evolutionary theory of Tielhard de Chardin

REALITY-LABYRINTH An emic reality created by the total structure of a language, mathematical system, artistic discipline, etc. A meta-structure made up of many interlocking reality-tunnels; a Paradigm.

REALITY-TUNNEL An emic reality established by a vivid metaphor and transmitted through symbolism across generations.

SEMANTICS The historical study of comparative reality-tunnels and reality-labyrinths.

WEALTH That part of the noösphere physically and tangibly present as artifacts or material structures.

Ronin Books for Independent Minds

PSYCHEDELIC PRAYERS_____Leary PSYPRA **12.95** ___
Guide to Transcendental experience based on the Tao Te Ching
HIGH PRIEST   Leary HIGPRI **19.95** ___
Acid trips with Huxley, Ginsburg, Burroughs, Ram Dass
CHAOS AND CYBER CULTURE   Leary CHACYB **35.00** ___
Cyberpunk manifesto on designing chaos and fashioning personal disorders
POLITICS OF ECSTASY   Leary POLECS **14.95** ___
Leary classic psychedelic writings that sparked the 60's revolution
PSYCHEDELICS ENCYCLOPEDIA   Stafford PSYENC **38.95** ___
Fascinating historical reference - from LSD to designer mind enhancers.
SCIENTIST   Lilly SCIENT **14.95** ___
Inside story of John C Lilly, M.D.'s life.
THE FUGIIVE PHILOSOPHER   Leary FUGPHI **12.95** ___
Philosophers ask questions. Auto-mobile! Joy-ride your body!
ILLUMINATI PAPERS   Wilson ILLPAP **14.95**___
Robert Anton Wilson's cosmic conspiracy
BRAIN BOOSTERS   Potter/Orfali BRABOO **16.95** ___
Improve mental performance w/ pharmaceuticals & vitamins, supplier list
CYBERPUNKS CYBERFREEDOM   Leary CYBPUN **12.95** ___
Reboot your brain, change reality screens. CyberPunk Manifesto
DISCORDIA   DISCORD **15.00** ___
HAIL Eris, Goddess of Chaos and Confusion. Religious spoof.
WAY OF THE RONIN   Potter WAYRON **14.95** ___
Riding the waves of change at work, cyberpunk career strategies

Books prices: SUBTOTAL $_____

CALIF customers add sales tax 8.75% _____

BASIC SHIPPING: (All orders)   **$6.00**

+ SHIPPING=> USA+$1/bk, Canada+$2/bk, Europe+$5/bk, Pacific+$7/bk_____
Books + Tax + Basic + Shipping: TOTAL $_____

M ake checks payable to **Ronin Publishing**

MC _ Visa _   Exp date _ _ / _ _ card #: _ _ _ _ _ _ _ _ _ _ _ _ _ _ _ _ _

(sign) _ _ _ _ _ _ _ _ _ _ _ _ _ _ _ Name_ _ _ _ _ _ _ _ _ _ _ _ _ _ _ _ _ _

Address _ _ _ _ _ _ _ _ _ _ _ _ _ _ City _ _ _ _ _ _ _ _ State _ _ ZIP_ _ _ _ _

Orders (800) 858-2665 • Info (510) 420-3670 • Fax (510) 420-3672
Ronin Publishing • Box 22900 • Oakland CA 94609
Stores & Distributors — Call for Wholesale info and catalog
Call for FREE catalog or go to web site **www.roninpub.com**

PRICE & AVAILABILITY SUBJECT TO CHANGE WITHOUT NOTICE.